drawing calm

RELAX, REFRESH, REFOCUS

with 20 Drawing, Painting, and Collage Workshops
Inspired by Klimt, Klee, Monet, and More

SUSAN EVENSON

QUARRY

Inspiring | Educating | Creating | Entertaining

Brimming with creative inspiration, how-to projects, and useful information to enrich your everyday life, Quarto Knows is a favorite destination for those pursuing their interests and passions. Visit our site and dig deeper with our books into your area of interest: Quarto Creates, Quarto Cooks, Quarto Homes, Quarto Lives, Quarto Drives, Quarto Explores, Quarto Gifts, or Quarto Kids.

© 2017 Quarto Publishing Group USA Inc.

Original artwork and project designs
© 2017 Susan Evenson

First published in 2017 by
Quarry Books, an imprint of
Quarto Publishing Group USA Inc.
100 Cummings Center
Suite 265-D
Beverly, Massachusetts 01915 USA
Telephone: (978) 282-9590
Fax: (978) 283-2742
QuartoKnows.com

Quarry Books titles are also available at discount for retail, wholesale, promotional, and bulk purchase. For details, contact the Special Sales Manager by email at specialsales@quarto.com or by mail at The Quarto Group, Attn: Special Sales Manager, 100 Cummings Center, Suite 265-D, Beverly, MA 01915, USA.

10 9 8 7 6 5 4 3 2 1

ISBN: 978-0-7603-7097-1
Digital edition published in 2017.

Library of Congress Cataloging-in-Publication Data

Names: Evenson, Susan, author.
Title: Drawing calm : relax, refresh, refocus with 20 drawing, painting, and
   collage workshops inspired by Klimt, Klee, Monet, and more / Susan Evenson.
Description: Beverly, Massachussetts : Quarry Books, 2017.
Identifiers: LCCN 2016043489 | ISBN 9781631591488 (paperback)
Subjects: LCSH: Art--Technique. | Art--Psychology. | BISAC: ART / Techniques
   / Drawing. | ART / Techniques / Watercolor Painting. | SELF-HELP /
   Creativity.
Classification: LCC N7433 .E94 2017 | DDC 701/.15--dc23
LC record available at https://lccn.loc.gov/2016043489
Book Design and Layout: Debbie Berne
Cover Image and Photography: Susan Evenson

Printed in Singapore

The information in this book is for educational purposes only. It is not intended to replace the advice of a physician or medical practitioner. Please see your healthcare provider before beginning any new health program.

For my family, friends, and teachers, and those who are all three. With an extra grateful heart for Tegan, Rocket, and Ryan. This book is for anyone who is looking for a bit of artful calm—whatever your version of that may be.

CONTENTS

FOREWORD

by Mary Rockwood Lane

Even before I began my career in nursing and teaching, I knew there were ways that we could help heal ourselves—and creativity was one of them. The focus and shedding of self-consciousness that goes into the creative process helps us step away from ourselves and untangle the everyday concerns that weigh us down. The pleasure that comes from making something with our hands, immersing ourselves in color, and creating something that wasn't there before—that truly reflects ourselves—lifts us like almost nothing else can.

In the years that I've worked with patients and with the University of Florida Arts in Medicine program, I've seen my earlier thoughts confirmed a thousand times over. Creating art is a process of renewal, not just for patients, but for all of us. Looking at art inspires. It helps us think outside ourselves and, in the process, to rediscover the best of who we are. When we reclaim our inner artist, the inner healer emerges, too—it's a force that lets the spirit take flight, and it spreads into every aspect of our lives, renewing our energy and self-esteem, while helping us discover our hidden gifts. That is what this book is about.

Drawing Calm brings art and renewal to life in ways that are accessible to everyone. It's a guide to finding creative time for you, however brief, each day through simple steps and inspiring art. It's a path to a new beginning, the start of a refreshing journey into the mind and spirit.

When I get started on a creative project, I like to begin by centering myself. Try it as you begin the projects in this book. It's simple, just take a moment to settle into your body and breathe deeply. Gently relax your entire body. In your mind's eye, focus on the area around your heart. Breathe into your heart, feeling deep appreciation for someone or something you love. Allow this feeling to spread through your entire body. The body will begin to feel

calmer as the heart opens. This is an invitation to create, to be inspired and let whatever emerges flow. Take the time to step away from the busy demands and stress of your life, and never forget—all of us are artists.

Mary Rockwood Lane, Ph.D., R.N., is an associate professor at the University of Florida College of Nursing, and associate faculty with the Watson Caring Science Institute, working in the field of creativity and spirituality in healing. She is cofounder and director emeritus of the Shands Arts in Medicine program at the University of Florida. She is the author of four books with Michael Samuels, M.D., including *Healing with the Arts, Creative Healing, The Path of the Feather*, and *Spirit Body Healing*.

"I found I could say things with colors and shapes that I couldn't say any other way— things I had no words for." —Georgia O'Keeffe

INTRODUCTION

Maybe it's because of a painting's rich palette, or the pattern of its brushstrokes, or the peace of a landscape view, but our response to art is often one of calm. Art can create a focal point for thought, inspire feelings of well-being, foster compelling conversations, and inspire us to create something ourselves. This book, part oasis, part journey, is a guide to getting there.

When we were young, creativity came naturally to us, arising from our curiosity, our sense of discovery, and our readiness to make things without knowing or caring what the end result would be. "Look what I made!" was always a joyful announcement, buoyed by a warm sense of accomplishment.

Many of us lose touch with that spontaneous drive as we get older. But losing touch doesn't mean that the urge to create and feel that warm place inside us isn't still there. We just need to make time for it.

The physical and psychological benefits of creativity in our lives are real. As you will see, the commentary throughout this book by noted author Mary Rockwood Lane, Ph.D., R.N., helps to explain the dynamics of why we respond to art the way that we do. Rolling up your sleeves and getting lost in creativity will help you feel that response.

We're all only too aware of how busy our lives are. Especially now, with so much emphasis on staying connected, the constant tug on our time can feel overwhelming. More than ever, we need to find our personal go-to "tools" that help us navigate the day and bring us back to center, reminding us of what's really important.

Creativity is very definitely one of those tools. The process of making something, choosing colors, and following where they lead us is both calming and exhilarating. Discovering our creativity allows us to discover some of the best parts of ourselves. That's what this book is about. It doesn't matter whether you have a talent for painting or any training in art at all. All you need is the desire to create and a little place in your life to make it happen.

No doubt about it, it can be hard to feel inspired to create art at the end of a work day—to find the energy to dream up new ideas and put them down on

paper. That's why each chapter in this book includes paintings by known artists as inspiration. These works by Monet, Redon, Klimt, and others, embody a refreshing sense of calm through colors and moods that suggest quiet, warmth, harmony, light, and reflection. Beginning with these sources of inspiration, I'll guide you step by step through the process of creating art projects in collage, paint, pencil, and pastels. But my projects truly are only a starting point. You can take the ideas and inspiration in any direction you choose.

Try to find time for yourself and your creativity every day. Let your imagination loose, and let your curiosity and sense of discovery rule.

—Susan Evenson

DRAWING CALM

GETTING STARTED

Time and Space and What You'll Need

You've decided you want to connect to art and to your creative self, but how do you make it happen? Can you book an hour or two on your calendar, or do you wait for a free afternoon? Do you creep downstairs when everyone is asleep late at night or get up before dawn?

The first step is to find your "you" time. Perhaps it's just a half hour every day, after the kids are in bed, or between the time when you get home from work and you plop mindlessly in front of the TV. Creative "you" time is precious and it's worth it to carve out a place for it in your day and protect it.

Once you do, let your family know that this is your special time and that it's important. Remind your friends not to phone you during that time. And don't just remind your family and friends—remind yourself. Getting into the groove of a new daily habit can take a bit of effort, but once you do, the benefits of your creative time will have a positive overflow into other parts of your life. As we all know, it's all too easy to give your time away. Dedicating time to yourself starts with the commitment.

Setting Up Your Workspace

Perhaps you already have a spot at home that's your haven for creative projects. The space doesn't need to be sprawling or even private. It just has to be a place where you can spread out your materials and leave them for the duration of the project. A corner of the kitchen table or a square of hardwood floor could be all you need.

If you have a separate room to call your own, you can leave your tools there, ready for you when you're ready for them. If you're working at the dining table, have a bin or two handy for storing your supplies and for easy set up.

None of the tools and materials used in this book are difficult to find. In fact, you probably have some of them in the house already. I've listed my favorite pens in the tools section for each project, but you may have your own favorites. Use what you enjoy—none of my suggestions are musts.

◄ *Field of Poppies*, Gustav Klimt, Austrian, (1862–1918). Oil on canvas, 1907. E. Lessing/Bridgeman Images.

Tools and Materials to Gather

Pencils—graphite pencils in any form. A set of colored pencils is a great addition.

Micron pens—these acid-free, archival pens will not bleed. Keep a few in varying thicknesses and colors on hand.

Watercolor paints—an inexpensive set from the craft store is just fine. Peerless makes great colors that are fun to use.

Drawing inks—these aren't a must, but they're great to play with, providing very saturated colors and beautiful washes.

Pastels—an inexpensive set is all you need.

Paintbrushes—collect a few in varying sizes, but nothing too tiny. You can start with an inexpensive variety pack and then buy more sizes as you need them.

Gesso is an acrylic paint used to prepare a surface (e.g., wood panels, canvas, and paper) to take different painting medium. It can help seal porous surfaces so that paint will adhere properly. **White gesso** is the most common, but gesso also comes in **black** and **clear**.

Matte medium is a liquid acrylic binder that can be used in collage or painting. It acts as glue in collage and can be applied with a paintbrush. It dries clear and matte. Matte medium can also be used to extend or thin acrylic paint.

Brush pens—start with a set or simply choose one or two colors that you like.

Gelly Roll pens—one or two in white.

Catalogs, magazines, and **junk mail** for collaging.

A ream of **white printer paper**, any size.

A pad of **mixed-media paper**, thick enough to stand up to watercolor painting and collage.

A few **canvas boards**, 11" × 14" (28 × 35.5 cm) or smaller.

Tissue paper in various colors. Be sure not to purchase the tissue paper with waxy coating.

A **hole punch**—standard is fine, but if you have other sizes, you'll find uses for them.

A **brayer** is a small, handheld roller used to spread paint or ink onto a surface.

A **glue stick or white glue** that you can apply with a brush.

Your Soundtrack

Jazz? Classical? What's your preference? Music can be a great way to change gears, set the mood, and start a task. If music helps you focus, then make sure there's music available in your creative space. Whether you stream music on your computer or create a specific playlist that signals the start of a project, have it ready to go. On the other hand, if silence works best for you, that's the way to go. Tune in to what you need.

The Fine Details

Are there other rituals that help you to focus? Whether you like to take a few deep breaths, make a cup of Earl Grey in your favorite mug, or bring a flower or rock inside from the garden, find little things that help you to settle in. Maybe you like to set up all of your tools and materials in an organized way or put on a special apron or scarf. All of these seemingly tiny details can add up to something special, unlocking the space that allows your creative time to unfold. Try to anticipate what you might need, and have those things close at hand.

Set your phone to vibrate and place it out of arm's reach. It can be so very tempting to let your phone distract you. Plan for this and do what you need to do to lessen the urge. This is your time and your experience. If there is anything else that helps you get settled in and stay focused, by all means, include it.

Creative Repose, by Mary Rockwood Lane

There's a reason why we come up with our best ideas and solutions after we've gone to bed—or even while we are asleep in the middle of the night. Studies show that the mind is its most creative when it's in repose, with the freedom to roam in all directions, explore at leisure, and make interesting connections. You can't do that when your mind is frantically busy with work and family issues. Setting aside a little corner of your home where you can be quiet and set your mind free to wander will allow your creative thoughts and solutions to come to life, even in bright daylight.

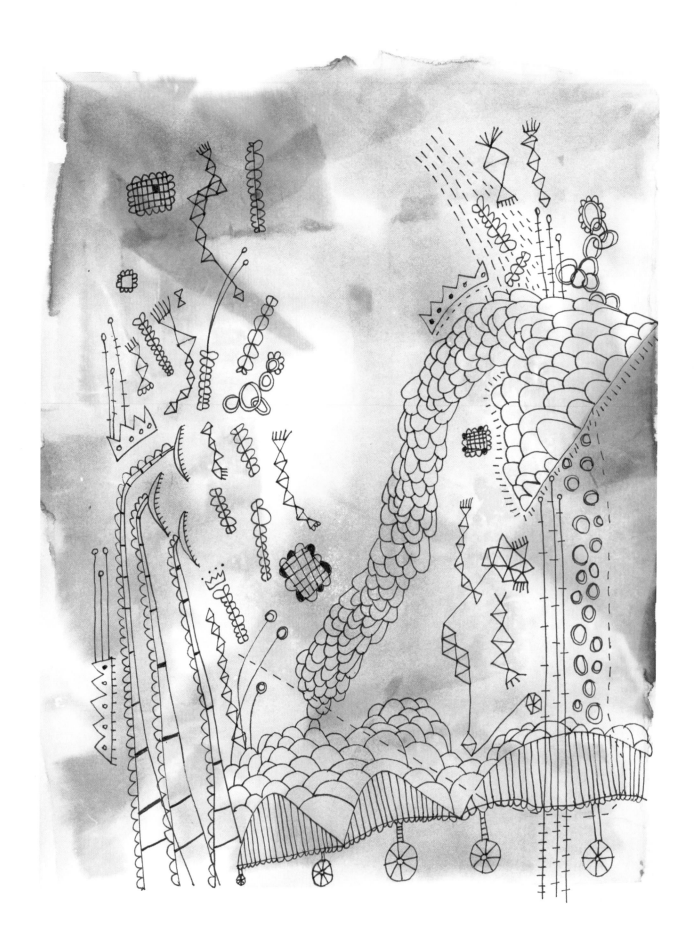

CHAPTER 1

WARM-UP EXERCISES

We stretch before running and warm up before jumping into challenging yoga postures. It also makes sense to warm up for creative time. These suggested exercises will allow you to transition from busy to calm and help you tune in to creative, open thinking.

You might find yourself doing one or two of these exercises before embarking on a project. Or maybe only one of the exercises resonates with you, and you do the same one each time. There is no right or wrong way to use the exercises, and they aren't all art projects. But all of them are designed with a similar spirit, intending to help you unwind and get your imagination flowing. As you let go of what the outcome might be, you may find the most creative solutions!

You may see the benefits of this practice throughout your day, as you are constantly problem solving. Remember that these exercises are here for you to play with and to enjoy.

◀ **Tissue paper painting by Susan Evenson.**

DRAW YOUR GROCERY LIST

EXERCISE 1

YOU WILL NEED:

- sheets of printer paper, any size
- pencil, black Micron pen, or another drawing utensil
- grocery list
- colored pencils or watercolors, optional

This is a playful approach to a very practical thing. We use lists to help us get things done, and they are simple and unemotional. For this exercise, you'll make an alternative grocery list.

Without using words, fill a page with drawings that illustrate the items on your grocery list. Work from an actual list, a list of grocery staples from memory, or a fantasy grocery list full of things you might like to buy but probably won't. There is only rule: no words.

Make your list with images. Be as playful as you can with it. Allow your imagination to kick in. As long as you can understand and interpret your list, you are doing great. Draw in pencil or pen, using whatever feels the best to you. Add color if you'd like. Draw like no one is watching! (They aren't, I promise!)

MAKE YOUR MARKS

YOU WILL NEED:

- sheets of printer or other paper, any size
- graphite and/or colored pencils
- black Micron, ballpoint, felt tip, or brush pens, your choice
- watercolor paints and paintbrushes, optional

This exercise is all about mark making. Choose one pen or pencil and a single sheet of paper and make twenty different kinds of marks on the page. Experiment with long, short, thin, thick, curvy, and straight marks. See what feels pleasurable to draw as well as what pleases you visually. Consider it an experiment for getting everything you can out of that particular pen or pencil.

After you fill the page, start again with a fresh piece of paper and allow yourself to expand your range of drawing tools. Continue exploring the different kinds of marks you can make, but this time switch up your pen every now and then. Experiment with watercolor, playing with the amount of water and size of brush to find out what kinds of brushstrokes you enjoy the most.

Notice how different pens or brushes feel in your hand and what kinds of marks spill out on the page. Play a little bit and see what happens. Do some marks seem to want to be drawn rapidly and repeated often? Do some marks slow you down and make you want to take your time? Enjoy the process of discovery and mark making.

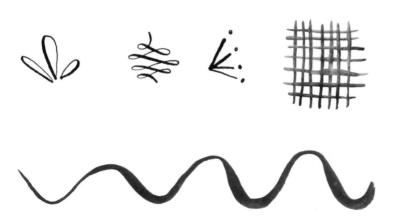

TISSUE PAPER PAINTING

This exercise is simple and relaxing. The finished pages are soft and pleasing to look at the way they are, but you can also use them as backgrounds for drawings or doodles. You may find that you start with your page one way, but end up flipping it around to find the right visual orientation once the tissue paper has been peeled away. Play with different color palettes, different sizes of ripped paper, and any other variable that you'd like to. One note on tissue paper—stay away from tissue paper that has a waxy coating because the color will not bleed onto your background paper.

YOU WILL NEED:

- tissue paper in your choice of colors and sizes
- scissors, optional
- sheet of watercolor paper or white card stock, 8″ x 10″ (20.5 x 25.5 cm)
- paintbrush
- cup of water
- black ballpoint or Micron pen, optional

1 Cut or tear the tissue paper into pieces, but not too small.

2 Put one piece on a sheet of watercolor paper. Brush water over the tissue paper, so that it stays put. Add bits of tissue paper one by one in the same way, overlapping the pieces if you like, until the sheet of paper begins to fill. Notice how the color in the tissue paper bleeds—it can lead to a beautiful effect.

   If you're happy with the piece as it is, call it done! Brushing a layer of matte medium over the piece will protect it and ensure that the tissue pieces stay put. If you want to experiment further, continue to step 3. (See A.)

3 Allow the collage to dry thoroughly. When it's dry, peel off the tissue paper. It will leave color behind, mimicking watercolor. (See B.)

4 If you like, go back into your creation with a pen and doodle on it. The next time you try this exercise, play around with your color palette. (See C.)

A

B

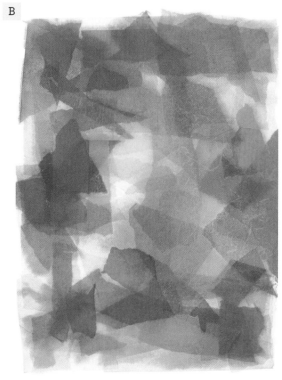

C

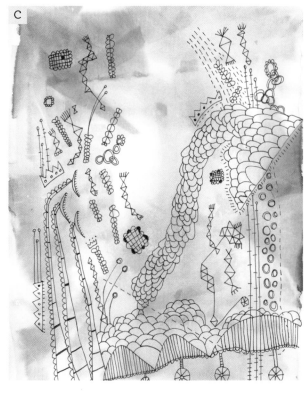

EXERCISE 4

TWENTY-FIVE TREES

Even though this exercise is called Twenty-Five Trees, you can substitute anything for the trees. The project is designed to have you think about something simple in a variety of ways. When you read the word "tree," one version of a tree probably comes to mind. That will be your starting point. Use this exercise to loosen up and change your way of thinking, or to shift gears, pique your curiosity, and play with an idea.

YOU WILL NEED:

- sheets of copy paper, any size
- pens, colored pencils, markers
- 25 index cards, any size

1   Gather your materials and start doodling on the copy paper. Think of the word "tree" and note what's in your mind. Draw that tree on your first index card. Use any mark-making materials you'd like, and don't spend too much time perfecting it.

2   Go back to your copy paper and doodle on it. Now make a new tree on the next index card. It can't be identical to the first tree. Make this one different. Change the tools you're using, the size of the tree, the kinds of leaves, and any other details you can imagine.

3   By this time, you're probably starting to open up, finding funny ways to differentiate one tree from another. Play and invent, drawing until you have twenty-five different trees on your index cards.

4   Turn the cards over and doodle drawings of trees on the other side, or choose another subject for twenty-five drawings. It could be something as simple as a circle or something more complex, such as birds or bugs. Play, explore, and note that making doodles of *anything* twenty-five times will change your perspective.

Although these are meant to be quick warm-ups, there's always room for embellishment later. (Add detail to the leaves, draw grass at the base of the tree, and so on.). Or, use what you've discovered as a jumping off point for another project. Stay open and see where your doodles take you.

DREAM HOUSE DOODLE

Using your imagination and creativity is easy when you want to fantasize about things that seem somewhat out of reach. Have you ever thought about what your dream home might be like? When money is no object and reality (or even gravity!) is not a concern, what kinds of details can you dream up? Have fun imagining the possibly impossible.

YOU WILL NEED:

- sheets of copy paper, any size
- pens and pencils
- watercolor paint, optional

1   Gather your materials and start imagining your dream house. Try to dream up ten different features for your house. They could be specific to you and your habits or something that you saw in a futuristic cartoon—they could be anything. Don't limit yourself by what is actually possible. Let your mind wander and give yourself endless possibilities. Get silly, get serious, or just let your curiosity rule with "what if?" questions.

2   List your ten dream house details on paper. As you do so, you might make a quick sketch of the details. Fill your pages with words and doodles, all working toward creating your perfect space.

3   You may find that these ideas prompt more detailed drawings or paintings. Explore them on paper if you like. Are you thinking about what your garden looks like? Or what color the house will be? What kind of location and atmosphere surrounds the house? No detail is too small or unimportant.

Have fun with it. This is all for you, and you don't have to stop at ten features—keep going and be as specific as you like. Your imagination is all you need to shift yourself out of rigid ways of thinking or away from a not-so-great day. Take the time to play and use your openness to explore more doodles and descriptions.

CHAPTER 2

DELIGHT

When I think of how it feels to look at art that resonates, as well as to make art that feels right, the word "delight" comes to mind. When something delights you visually, it brings a smile to your face or it makes you feel good. Does it feel amusing, charming, or remind you of something personal? Delight has a joyful component to it and it's a wonderful feeling to meditate on, spend time in, and make art from. You can't edit what you feel is delightful, it just is. Perhaps it's a color combination, the quality of a line or brushstroke, or the way shapes are juxtaposed on a page. It's a personal response, and it just feels good to play with the idea and the sense of delight.

◄ *Reward of Merit (Belohnung),* Fraktur painting, American School. Pen and ink with watercolor on paper, nineteenth century. Free Library, Philadelphia/Bridgeman Images.

DRAWING CALM

FLOWERS, FLOWERS, EVERYWHERE

This project is about delight in floral form. It's impossible to look at a field of flowers and the refreshing greens of leaves and grass without feeling a sense of calm and pleasure. What I love about Klimt's flowers for this project is his melodic rhythm of simple, repeated shapes and the unfussy way that he caught the feel of flowers in a field. Because your eyes don't have to focus on floral details, they can just enjoy the refreshing use of color. Use Klimt's painting as a reference, find a picture in a magazine, or use your own garden for inspiration. We'll make a field of flowers in a color palette of your choosing.

YOU WILL NEED:

- 11" x 14" (28 x 35.5 cm) canvas, canvas board, or primed wood panel
- acrylic or gouache paints
- paintbrushes, in a variety of sizes
- flowers from your garden, photos of flowers from the internet, or flowers from your own imagination
- sketch paper and pencil, optional

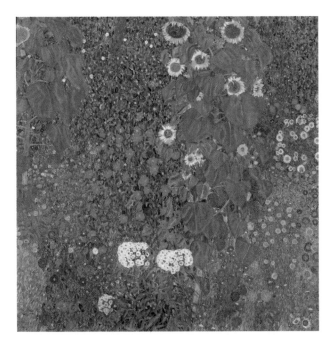

Farm Garden with Sunflowers, Gustav Klimt, Austrian (1862–1918). Oil on canvas, 1905–06. Osterreichische Galerie Belvedere, Vienna/Bridgeman Images.

Field of Poppies, Gustav Klimt, Austrian (1862–1918). Oil on canvas, 1907. E. Lessing/Bridgeman Images.

1 Create a surface for your flowers. Start by painting the canvas with a pale green or green and yellow base. Then go back and stipple in areas of darker green. (See A.)

2 While the background dries, think about the colors and varieties of flowers you'd like to see in your green field. I've used a simple red, white, and blue color scheme, but you could make your garden every color in the rainbow. If it helps, test your ideas by making pencil sketches of your flowers on a piece of paper, reducing them to their simplest forms.

3 Think about the composition for your painting. In *Field of Poppies*, Klimt sprinkled flowers throughout, with a horizon line and trees at the top. In *Garden with Sunflowers*, he made a pyramid shape of flowers that reaches to the top of the painting. Use either approach as inspiration for your painting or invent your own composition. (See B.)

4 Add your flowers. I've painted mine as simple circles and asterisk shapes that are easy to repeat. Vary the colors so that your field appears to have sunlit spots and shadows. (See C.)

5 It's time to unify your flowers. Choose a detail that will provide a common link. Do you want each one to have a yellow center? Maybe it's definition in the petals or stems or the addition of small, leafy shapes that ties the painting together. Highlights? Bright color in dark places? Sit back and enjoy your creation and consider an alternate palette for your next painting. (See D.)

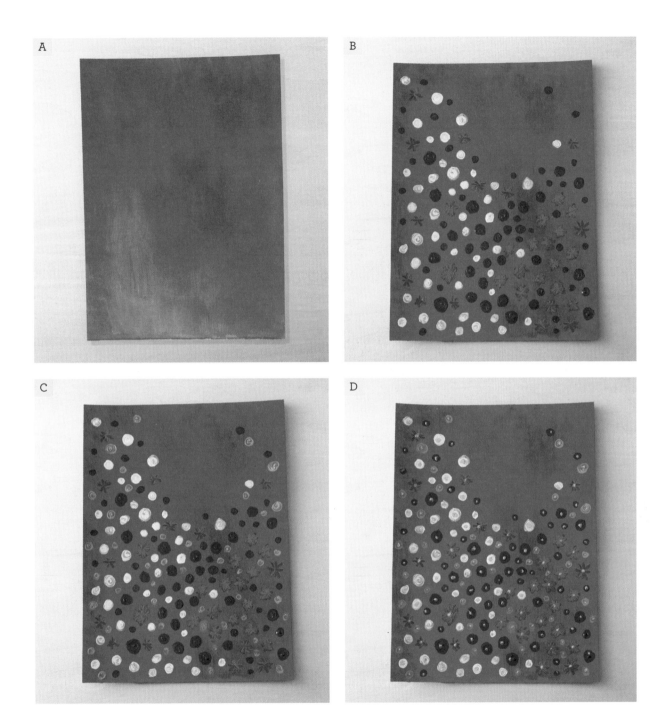

DRAWING CALM

PIZZA PAINTING

Sometimes just looking at the way an artist used brushstrokes freely in a painting can bring delight—you know the artist let go completely and was having fun with it.

Do you have a little nervous energy to get out? This project might be a good one for you. See what happens as you experiment with your own energetic mark making. Of course there's no real pizza involved, but you can imagine one and add beautiful, colorful layers of shapes as tasty toppings. Either gouache or acrylic paints work well for this project because they're opaque and allow you paint on top of the previous layers, once they've dried.

YOU WILL NEED:

- 11" x 14" (28 x 35.5 cm) canvas board, primed wood panel, or stretched canvas

- gouache or acrylic paints, including black and white

- paintbrushes, in a variety of sizes

- colored pencils

- white gesso

- graphite pencil

Parody of the Blue Knight, **August Macke, German (1887–1914). Oil on canvas, 1913. Stadtische Galerie im Lenbachhaus, Munich/ Bridgeman Images.**

1   Decide whether you'd like your drawing to be horizontal or vertical and place your canvas board in front of you. Start with a light palette. Mix a few tones of differing colors and begin painting the surface, making sure the colors stay light. Allow to dry. This is the sauce. (See A.)

2   Create a layer of squiggles with the black gouache and several different brush sizes. Play with the squiggles as you paint them, varying the length and shape. When you're happy with the variety on your page, stop and let the paint dry. Be sure to leave some light background peeking through for contrast. We'll call this the cheese layer. (See B.)

3   For the third layer, choose a few colors (a shade each of red and green and a shade or two of blue) and scatter some shapes on top of the squiggles. Consider a few different ovals and long wobbly lines—whatever strikes your mood. This is the toppings layer. Let these larger shapes unify the painting. (See C.)

4   For the top layer, add white highlights. Thin some white gouache with a little water to make it slightly transparent. Brush it onto the painting wherever you'd like highlights. The highlights will be bright spots on your painting. Allow them to cut through any gray areas or any areas that appear muddled.

5   Finally, you might go back into your painting and add pencil details. Tiny marks can provide contrast within shapes and create visual interest. Play with the idea of contrasts: little vs. big, straight vs. curvy, thin vs. thick, and so on. These nuances will help add interest and variation to your composition.

A

B

C

DRAWING CALM

TEXTURED FLOWERS

This project was inspired by Odilon Redon's pastel *Flowers*. It's a playful drawing in color, subject matter, and execution. The flowers are in a vase, but it's anything but rigid and fussy, and although the environment is nonspecific, light and shadows are suggested. You don't even have to think of his forms as flowers—just beautiful and surprising shapes and colors that combine happily like a puff of magic from a magician's wand. Working with similar subject matter and materials, create your own vase of flowers by experimenting with mark making. Play with the color and shapes until you're happy with your creation.

YOU WILL NEED:

- 11" x 14" (28 x 35.5 cm) piece of pastel or mixed-media paper
- pastels or chalk set
- colored pencils, graphite pencils, or markers
- spray fixative, optional

- white gesso
- paintbrush
- china marker, black crayon, and/or black pencil

Flowers, Odilon Redon, French (1840–1916). Pastel on paper, 1907–10. Private Collection/ Bridgeman Images.

1 Set the paper horizontally on a work surface. With the pastels, create a variegated surface as a background. Play with a limited palette. (Try whites, grays, and one or two contrasting colors.) Try to envision where your flowers will live once the ground is complete. You can use the composition in the Redon drawing as a starting point, but once you start, improvise. (See A.)

   Note: If the background gets muddy, spray the surface with a little fixative. When it dries, you'll be able to go back over the areas you've already worked and add clarity.

2 Add definition to your soft background. Be delicate in some areas and heavier in others. Use pencils or markers to enliven the surface and roughly indicate where the vase and flowers will be.

3 Paint a little white gesso on the surface. Focus the gesso around the vase and flower area, allowing some background color to peek through. (See B.)

4 Draw the flower shapes. You could use a flower from your yard as a model or from a photo you love. Don't fret about drawing it realistically. This is about capturing what drew you to it in the first place—was it color, shape, or the details in the center? (See C.)

5 Experiment with different ways of drawing the same flower, as loose as you'd like. Add details with the china marker or a black colored pencil.

6 Add a contrasting flower, leaf, or branch. Try different variations to accent the arrangement of flower colors. (See D.)

7 Anchor your bouquet with a vase, if you like, and then step back from your drawing and take a look. Are there areas that feel too busy? Consider going back into those areas to unify or soften your marks. Are there too many similar colors together? Go back in and add something fresh. (A little pop of yellow, pink, or red in a field of gray will add relief.) Different sizes and shapes of marks add interest to a neutral area. Take your time and finesse the details until you're happy with the way your drawing flows. (See E.)

Notes on multiples: In general, odd numbers create a more interesting composition than even numbers. Keep that in mind as you add flowers and leaves. The odd flower might be more visually pleasing than a balanced set of two.

Notes on composition: Direct the eye and create a focal point in your drawing by making the main subject area the most detailed and active part of the composition. Think of this as you prepare your background: you might want to keep anything too particular or active away from the edges of the page.

CHAPTER 3

QUIET

The word "quiet" can conjure images of a natural landscape, absent of the hum of the city. It can bring up colors that feel peaceful and hushed. Quiet can refer to the way it feels to observe a work of art or the state of mind of an artist. It can be your choice of a certain palette that feels still or even silent. We can easily link the words "quiet" and "calm." The projects in this section live in a quiet space, with moments of stillness and softness throughout.

◀ *Birch Tree*, William Turner (Turner of Oxford), (1789–1862). Gouache on paper, nineteenth century. Courtesy of the Warden and Scholars of New College, Oxford, UK/Bridgeman Images.

DRAWING CALM

GLOWING NIGHTSCAPE

This Norman Garstin painting captures a quiet moment of awe under a night sky full of radiant light. With the absence of people or animals, it creates a sense of peace and space.

I love using chalk and pastels when I play with creating atmospheric effects or glowing light. They draw beautifully on dark or toned paper, as here, for the feel of light in a night sky. They also blend, one into the next, easily with a fingertip or blending stick to create the fiery effects of the sunlight or stars.

YOU WILL NEED:

- 8″ x 10″ (20.5 x 25.5 cm) or 9″ x 12″ (23 x 30.5 cm) blue construction paper
- black colored pencil
- pastels or chalks
- white colored pencil
- blending stick or chamois

Aurora on the Prairie, Norman Garstin, Irish (1847–1926). Oil on panel, 1886. Private Collection/Bridgeman Images.

1 Place the paper on your work surface horizontally. Imagine it divided into thirds. The horizon line will be one third of the way up from the bottom of your page. This leaves the top two-thirds for the sky. Start by using your black pencil to draw the horizon line. If you like, define the horizon with treetops, hills, or the top of a house. Color the foreground to anchor the sense of place. (See A.)

2 The blue of the paper provides the base blue of the sky. (If you weren't able to find blue paper, create your sky with pastels.) Blend several blues and pearly grays to develop the sky. Use your finger, a chamois, or a blending stick to blend the blue tones. (See B.)

3 Add tiny white stars to the sky. (See C.)

4 Now create the glow. Sketch the arch of the aurora. Using the side of a white pastel, start at the lowest point of the arch and draw the pastel out to the edge of the page. Vary your pressure with each stroke so that there are lighter and darker areas. Let some of the blue paper and stars show through your veil of white. Add touches of gray or yellow to enhance the glow. (See D.)

5 Return to the stars and enhance them with another touch of white.

When you're done, try a similar drawing using the early morning sky as inspiration. Use yellow paper to start and blend the pink and orange colors of the sun.

Illumination, by Mary Rockwood Lane

In my own research, data has shown that when images of light and beauty emerge in someone's artwork, the artist reports feeling an enormous sense of peace. This is often accompanied by sensations of energy, buzzing, calmness, and joy. The feeling has been described as being within a "vortex of energy," exhilaration, and feeling fully alive.

Art creates feelings of self-worth and self-understanding. When you see yourself in this light, you can honor your intuitions and insights. You can be illuminated to find your place in the world.

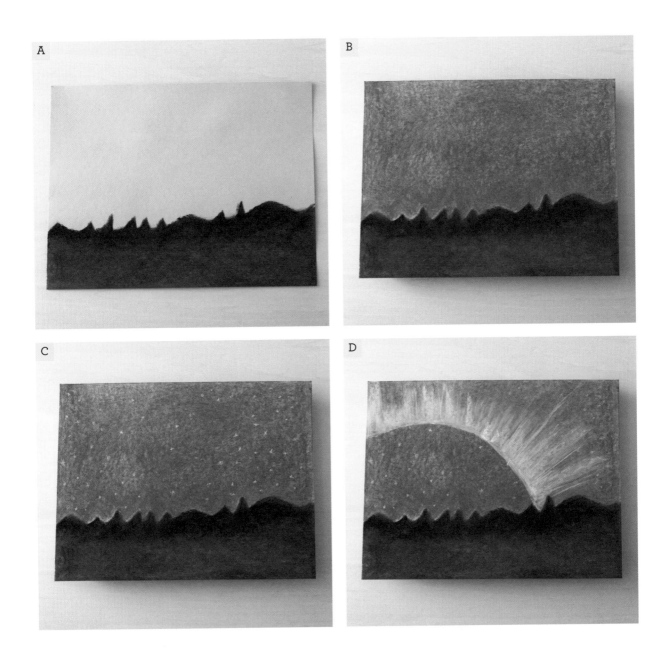

DRAWING CALM

LITTLE HOUSES

A horizon and sky, a lack of clutter, and clean, straight lines can create a sense of calm—there's no noise in this view. In *Landscape with Five Houses*, Kazimir Malevich has created a clean and quiet scene that we can use as a guide in creating a painted collage. Take a look at the foreground space, where the horizon line is, and how much sky you can see in his painting. Changing the depth of the foreground and distance to the houses can make the view feel cozier or cooler. We're going to play with the ratios of foreground and background, as well as collaging five houses onto the horizon line.

YOU WILL NEED:

- 9" x 12" (23 x 30.5 cm) stretched canvas, canvas board, or primed wood panel
- pencil
- acrylic paints
- paintbrushes, in a variety of sizes
- watercolor paper or Bristol (Scraps are fine.)
- scissors or craft knife
- white glue or matte medium
- colored pencils
- white gesso
- black Micron pens, in a variety of widths

Landscape with Five Houses, Kazimir Severinovich Malevich, Russian (1878–1935). Oil on canvas, c. 1932. State Russian Museum, St. Petersburg/ Bridgeman Images.

1   Place the canvas vertically on your work surface. Imagine your composition. Do you want the emphasis in the foreground? Do you want the sky to guide your finished work? Decide which area will take up the most space in your composition.

    Draw the horizon line with a pencil. If you want the houses to be the heroes of your composition, your horizon line will be low so that the height of the buildings will dominate. If you want the sky to be the focus, also set your horizon low. You might want only two small houses in your composition so that your sky will have plenty of breathing room. If you decide to have more play in the foreground, make the horizon line high, leaving just enough space for a few little houses and small amount of sky. (See A.)

2   Loosely plan your color palette. Find a range of warm tones for the foreground and a cooler color for the sky or background. (See B.)

3   Choose the colors that you want for your houses and roofs. Use the acrylics to paint watercolor paper with those colors. Make sure you have enough painted paper for five houses and five roofs. Add additional details or textures to the painted surfaces, or leave them as blocks of color. Allow the paint to dry completely. (See C.)

4   Cut the houses and roofs from the painted paper. Think about whether you'd like a line of similarly sized houses or if you'd like more variety. Play with the different sizes and shapes. (See D and E.)

5   Paint the foreground of your canvas a warm color. Use a flat color that you've mixed or varied tones of a single color. Your horizon can be a straight line or run diagonally, like a hill. (See F.)

6   Paint the sky a cool color. Clean up the horizon line if needed. While the paint dries, look at your composition and think about where you'll place the houses. (See G.)

7   Lay out the house bases and roofs on the canvas. Arrange them loosely until you find a configuration you like. You can stick to the original plan of five houses or find another number. Do you want to change the colors? Maybe there should be one pink house in a row of white ones. (See H.)

8   Glue the houses into place. Are they on the horizon or below it? Equidistant from each other or more randomly spaced? Perfectly perpendicular or tilting slightly? It's your landscape, you decide.

9   Finally, step back to see how your composition has come together. Does it need additional collaged paper pieces? Does it need black or white painted details to unify the composition? Perhaps you'll want to detail the houses with colored pencil or a Micron pen. (See I.)

When you're done, try another collage painting. You could use houses of different shapes or a more varied color palette. You could orient your canvas horizontally to see how that changes your approach. Play with the different variables, enjoy the materials, and relax into the process.

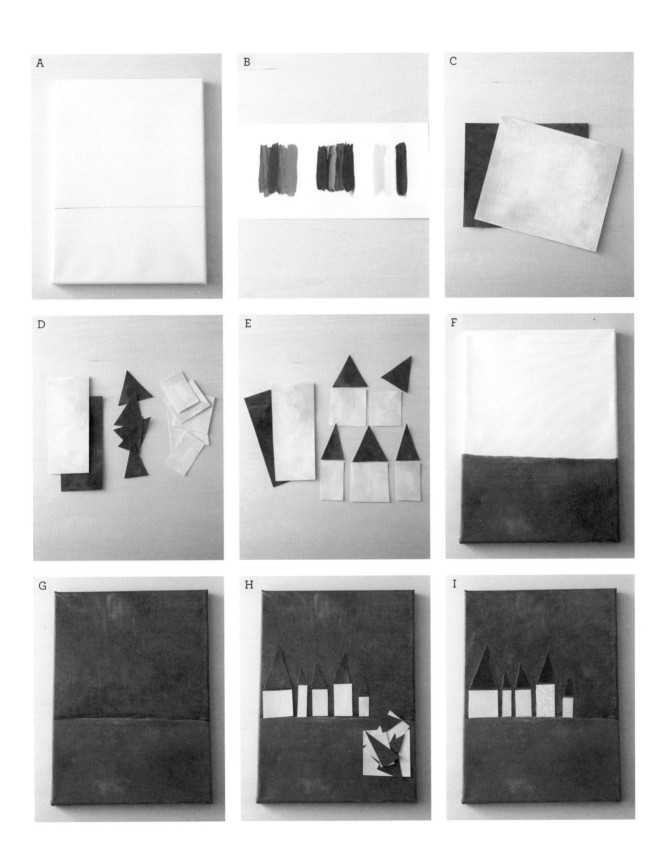

DRAWING CALM

SILENT BEACH

A beach offers a still point where we can let go of our busy schedules, clear our minds, and tune into nature. This Degas drawing has a wonderfully peaceful feel to it. What I love about it is that Degas created such a deep vista of sand, sea, and sky simply with horizontal bands of color. I've played with this idea, using torn strips of paper colored with watercolor and gouache, but you could try it with pastel. Allow for some ambiguity, as getting specific or busy can change the feel of the work entirely. Let your colors remain flowing and soft.

YOU WILL NEED:

- 8″ x 10″ (20.5 x 25.5 cm) or 9″ x 12″ (23 x 30.5 cm) Bristol board or watercolor paper
- three pieces of watercolor paper, 8″ x 10″ (20.5 x 25.5 cm)

- watercolors and gouache
- paintbrushes, in a variety of sizes
- water
- matte medium

Marine Sunset,
**Edgar Degas, French
(1834–1917). Pastel on
paper, c. 1869. Private
Collection/Bridgeman
Images.**

1   Imagine a seascape, using the Degas painting as a reference. Paint the Bristol board with a sand color. It can be an off-white or light brown, or lighter in some areas and darker in others. Allow the paint to dry completely. (See A.)

2   Paint the three pieces of watercolor paper, one in varying shades of blues, another with whites, and the third with soft yellow tones. Orient each of these horizontally on your workspace. (See B.)

3   Tear the painted sheets from step 2 into irregular horizontal strips. The paper can still be a little wet. There may be rough spots and crooked lines, which is okay. Enjoy the imperfections. (See C.)

4   Imagine a band of deep water at the bottom of the page, a brighter horizon line toward the middle, and a vast sky above. Overlap the pieces of torn paper on the background, brushing water over them to hold them together. Notice how you can add piece after piece to construct the three areas of color. The brightest band is in the center of the page. (See D.)

5   Attach the strips to the surface with matte medium. Starting at the bottom, attach the darkest section. Move up to the brightest area and then to the sky. Don't worry if the colors aren't coming together the way you want them quite yet. Let the matte medium dry. (See E.)

6   How do the bands of collaged color look? Do you have beautiful torn edges that are adding to the depth of the landscape? Add a few more torn pieces of painted paper, if you like.

7   Now focus on how the color is lying on the page. Do you need to add anything? Does it feel hazy and beautiful, or do you want richer color? You can go back in with paint now and work on any areas that need a little something more. Start with a watery paint and let the subtle colors and torn paper textures remain important elements on the page. Enjoy the subtlety of the sea, sky, and the beautiful textures you've created.

A

B

C

D

E

CHAPTER 4

WARMTH

Certain words connect instantly to a feeling, and warmth is one of them. Warmth reminds us of the feeling of snuggling in a cozy blanket, the way sunshine feels on our face, or of the golden light of a summer afternoon. These are all positive associations.

The projects in this section have a warm color palette in common. They come across in different ways, with different subject matter and compositions—but always with warmth.

"Art is a line around your thoughts."
—Gustav Klimt

◄ *Tree of Life*, Stoclet Frieze, Gustav Klimt, Austrian (1862–1918). Tempera and watercolor, c. 1905–09. MAK (Austrian Museum of Applied Arts) Vienna/Bridgeman Images.

BUTTERFLIES

This project takes inspiration from Odilon Redon's *Evocation of Butterflies*. He chose the colors that come to mind for most of us when we think of warmth—the glowing golds and oranges of a sunset or fireside. We'll develop a warm, rich painted surface, build it up, let it dry, and then add our focal point—butterflies or anything else you like—traveling across the page.

YOU WILL NEED:

- sketch pad or printer paper, any size
- graphite pencil
- reference material for your focal point
- 9" x 12" (23 x 30.5 cm) watercolor paper or Bristol board
- gouache
- watercolors
- paintbrushes, in a variety of sizes
- colored pencils
- white gesso

Evocation of Butterflies, Odilon Redon, French (1840–1916). Oil on canvas, c. 1912. Detroit Institute of Arts, USA/ Bridgeman Images.

1   Think about your subject for this exercise and let your mind wander. You can use butterflies as your focal point or another subject you enjoy. It could be flat, graphic symbols, such as hearts or circles, or something that you like to draw, such as flowers or trees.

    Work out the basics for your painting on the sketchpad. Draw from memory or gather reference material. Make as many drawings as you like, but don't get mired down with getting everything perfect. A loose plan will do.

2   Look through your paint colors and note the warmer colors—perhaps the ones you choose are rosier than Redon's. We'll build up the surface of the painting slowly, adding warm colors in layers. Start with light washes and larger brushstrokes. Add other colors and tones to create more depth on your page. Play with lights and darks, and note how each color you add affects the page. Drip paint, splatter your brush a bit, or employ any other active techniques you can. The goal is to be playful with your color palette. (See A.)

3   You may find after working loosely with paint that the orientation of your page doesn't feel right anymore. Go from vertical to horizontal and back again, if you like. Let the paint dry a bit and then go back in, adding more paint or perhaps areas of colored pencil to create fertile ground for your drawing. This step can take time. Don't rush. If you'd like, work on two background paintings at a time and choose your favorite for the drawing.

4   When the background is dry, plan your drawing. If you've chosen butterflies, decide how they'll fly across your page. Try five of them. The only rule is to not put the largest in the center of the page. If some background areas are too dark to draw on, lighten them with white gouache so your drawings can be seen. (Keep in mind that the white areas won't stay white.) (See B.)

5   Add details to your drawing. If you're drawing butterflies, will they each have a slightly different shape? Are they all flying in the same direction? Do they have spots, stripes, or other details? (See C.)

Concentration and Mindfulness, by Mary Rockwood Lane

When someone translates images into art, either by drawing, journaling, or playing music, these types of art activities produce a deep level of concentration and mindfulness. If the image is one of joy or release of tension, the body is put in a healing state through the hypothalamic pathways of the parasympathetic nervous system. Heartbeat and breathing slow, blood pressure drops, blood goes to the intestines, the whole body changes. This happens automatically. You don't need to do anything except to focus on the art. The neural pathways of the mind take over, and you're taken "elsewhere" to a mental state of pure concentration that most resembles meditation.

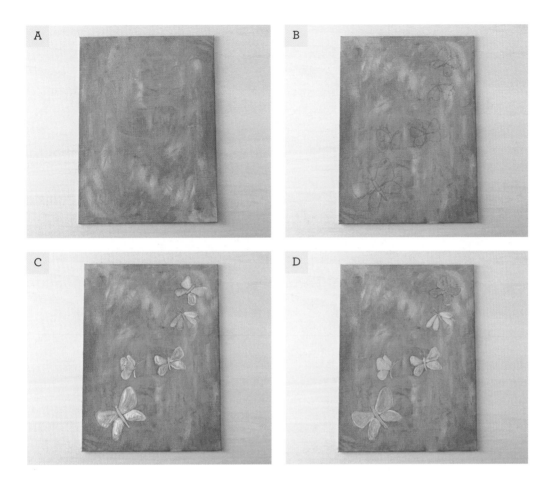

6   Keeping your warm palette in mind, add color to your drawing. Use the Redon painting as a starting point, or branch off in your own direction. You may want to start adding color with paint and then go back into each item with colored pencils.

7   Use tiny brushes or pencil to add any details and embellish any way you'd like. Try to make the transition from paint to colored pencils seamless. Experiment with color and how best to define your drawings. The goal isn't to be realistic, but to play with the materials and get the most out of them. (See D.)

8   Take a look at the page. How is your subject interacting with the background? Does the composition need more integration? Add some of the color from the focal points into the background. Do they feel too similar? Try outlining an edge or two to help them pop, or perhaps, deepen the background behind the items to help them stand out more. Once you're happy with your composition, allow it to dry.

Ready to try another? Create another background and then prepare it for drawing. Continue the subject that you started in your initial piece or choose a new one. Did you get too complex with the first? Simplify this one, using geometric shapes as your subject.

DRAWING CALM

TREE OF CALM

Trees are a wonderful subject for artists. While rooted in the earth, they reach up to the sky and can be stylized any way you'd like. Gustav Klimt made graphic, but flowing, decorative trees in many of his paintings. They are always full of interest. In this project, we'll make a tree of calm inspired by Klimt's *Tree of Life*.

YOU WILL NEED:

- 8″ x 10″ (20.5 x 25.5 cm) or 9″ x 12″ (23 x 30.5 cm) watercolor paper or Bristol board

- graphite and colored pencils

- pieces of cardboard to use for rolling paint

- acrylic paints

- brayer or paint roller

- scrap paper

- small paintbrushes

- card stock for cutting stencils

- craft knife

Tree of Life, Stoclet Frieze, detail of the left-hand side, Gustav Klimt, Austrian (1862–1918). Tempera and watercolor, c. 1905–09. MAK (Austrian Museum of Applied Arts) Vienna/Bridgeman Images.

1   Choose your preferred color palette. (See A.)

2   Set out the sheet of watercolor paper and mark the horizon line with a pencil. Squeeze out and mix your darkest background color on the piece of cardboard. Use the brayer to roll the color onto the watercolor paper. Add a little white or black to the color for variance while you're rolling—it's best if there are a variety of tones. Cover the page completely with this color and allow it to dry. (See B.)

3   Mix and roll out your lighter color(s) on a piece of cardboard with the brayer. Apply the lighter color above the horizon. (See C.)

4   Now imagine your tree. Draw a few kinds of trees on the scrap paper until you find a style that appeals to you. Do you like twisty branches or straight ones? A thinner trunk or a sturdier one? Look outside, in books, or explore the internet to find tree shapes that you like. We aren't looking for a very realistic tree, but more of an iconic representation of trunk, branches, and leaves. (See D.)

5   After making doodles on your scrap paper, use a pencil to lightly draw the general shape of the trunk and branches on your painted background. Don't worry about the leaves yet. (See E.)

6   Using your darker background color and a small brush, paint the trunk and branches. Feel free to improvise from your sketch. You may decide that you want more branches, longer branches, or perhaps you've thought of a completely new way to draw a tree you love. Allow the paint to dry completely. (See F.)

7   What style of leaves would you like? They can be any shape. Klimt used triangles for leaves on one of one his trees (see page 52), which is not a typical leaf shape. Sketch some possibilities on your scrap paper. Draw your favorite shapes in a variety of sizes onto a piece of card stock.

8   Carefully cut the leaf shapes from the card stock. You will use these as stencils. (See G.)

9   Choose a few colors for the leaves. Without too much planning, use a brush to apply paint through the leaf stencils. Vary the size and color of the leaves. You may wish to stencil the leaves in stages, allowing them to dry in between. Take it bit by bit. Maybe you'd like to see areas of dense leaves, contrasted with lighter areas, or perhaps, you like a more uniform look. (See H.)

10 When the leaves are dry, use a paintbrush to add any additional details or embellishment. Do you want to add any details to the leaves? Do you want a bug crawling on the ground next to your tree or small flowers at the tree's base?

11 Finally, within the leaves, the trunk, or in the background, find places where you can add touches of white. Use Klimt's paintings as inspiration, or come up with your own method.

12 Take one more look at your painting. Does it seem complete or could it use something more? If there are any final adjustments to make, go back in and work on them. When you're ready to call your first tree of calm done, begin new trees to create an entire forest of calm.

A

B

C

D

E

F

G

H

HAYSTACK HOUSE

Monet's *Haystacks at Sunset* absolutely glows with warmth. His haystack almost looks like a small cottage facing the setting sun. In fact, that was the inspiration for this project. In doing our watercolor, we'll change the haystack to a house. With this project, you can imagine yourself moving into Monet's landscape in a cozy sunlit cottage of your own. Even if you are not familiar with drawing houses, try drawing a house from your imagination. It doesn't need to be detailed, so don't worry about your drawing skills, or rendering anything perfectly. Keep it simple.

YOU WILL NEED:

- sketchbook or paper, any size
- pencil
- 8" x 10" (20.5 x 25.5 cm) canvas board, stretched canvas, or primed panel
- watercolor paints
- gouache

- paintbrushes
- white gesso
- black gesso
- white colored pencil
- black colored pencil

Haystacks at Sunset, Frosty Weather, Claude Monet, French (1840–1926). Oil on canvas, 1891. Private Collection/ Bridgeman Images.

1   In the sketchbook, make a doodle of a simple house. Keep it as simple as a square and a triangle, if you like, or any other version of a house that speaks to you. (See A.)

2   Place the canvas board horizontally on your workspace. Use a pencil to divide the surface into the three horizontal bands—foreground, background, and sky. Decide where you'd like to place your house and sketch it simply. You can follow Monet's lead with the location of his haystack, or come up with your own spot. My only instruction is to keep your house out of the exact center of the page. (See B.)

3   Use watercolors to play with color on the sketchpad. A warm color palette is typically rich with yellow and can include different shades of reds and oranges, as well. Use cooler colors, such as blues and greens, for contrast. (See C.)

4   Begin with the sky. In Monet's painting, the sky is the lightest section, but it isn't a bright white—yellows, oranges, and pinks enhance it. Play with the idea of making one side of the painting darker and the other side lighter. (See D.)

5   Next, move to the background, the darkest part of the composition. Make brushstrokes using many colors in your palette to help unify the composition. If your house is going to interrupt the background, leave space where the house will be. You can refine the edges later. (See E.)

6   The foreground is lighter, but not as light as the sky. Continue to unify the sections with brushstrokes of common colors throughout. (See F.)

7   Start painting the house with rich, warm oranges, yellows, and pinks that stand out on the page. Differentiate the color of the roof from the lower part of the house for contrast and readability. Add shadow at the base of the house. Add brushstrokes of cooler tones in the shadows to separate them from the house itself. You can leave the house loosely painted, like Monet's haystack, or add more details, such as a door, windows, and a shingled roof. (See G.)

8   Clean up the areas where one section meets another. If you'd like, go back in with colored pencils to define areas. Play with the edges a bit until all the elements are balanced and working together. Then sit back and enjoy the view of your little house. Can you feel the warmth? (See H.)

A

B

C

D

E

F

G

H

CHAPTER 5

HARMONY

We are familiar with the word "harmony" linked with music. Listening to vocalists harmonizing or hearing a certain chord played can be so pleasing. But we also experience visual harmony, which can give us a feeling of balance and peace. Harmony occurs when all of the elements being played with work together—nothing feels overworked and all is well with the world. In this chapter, we'll explore projects based on the idea of harmony. Notice the elements that help tie things together and when a small adjustment helps to tell a story. Harmonize your colors, your composition, and your subject matter, and see what happens to the art-making process as you go.

◄ *The Talisman*, or *The Swallow-hole in the Bois d'Amour, Pont-Aven*, Paul Serusier, French (1864–1927). Oil on panel, 1888. Musée d'Orsay, Paris/Bridgeman Images.

DRAWING CALM

RAINBOW DROPS

Rainbows always catch us unaware when they appear out of nowhere in the sky. Ephemeral marvels of color, they are the perfect symbol of harmony, formed when the elements of light and moisture line up perfectly to make something beautiful and new. No wonder they seem to carry messages of hope, luck, happiness, and good days to come. Create your own rainbow with the colors of the spectrum or any harmonious colors of your choice.

YOU WILL NEED:

- watercolor paints
- paintbrushes, in a variety of sizes
- plate to use as a palette
- 8″ x 10″ (20.5 cm x 25.5 cm) sheets of watercolor paper
- scrap watercolor paper for testing your colors

Sky Study with Rainbow, John Constable, British (1776–1837). Watercolor on paper, 1827. Yale Center for British Art, Paul Mellon Collection, USA/ Bridgeman Images.

1   Choose a color palette that you want to explore. You might use a series of blues with a contrasting gold or yellow or the rainbow in the reference painting as a guide. Find three or more colors to play with, mix them, and have them ready on your palette. (See A.)

2   Set a piece of watercolor paper vertically in front of you on your work surface. Wet your brush and let a few drops of your darkest color fall at the top edge of the paper. Tilt it at various angles to encourage the paint to slide down the page, perhaps in the arc of a rainbow. If the color isn't dark enough, add another pass with the same color. If you're happy with your first drip, allow it to set up and almost dry before introducing your next color. You can guide the drips with your brush, or blot them with a paper towel and go back in with more watercolor. (See B.)

3   Using the second darkest color, start at the top of the page again and add a new drip near the first. Make decisions as you go along, adding more of the second color or letting it dry and switching to the third. You can create your rainbow as wide as you'd like, with as many colors as you'd like, going in any direction you prefer. (See C and D.)

4   Take a look at your page. Did the colors run into one another? Are there drips you want to clean up? Add a background with thinned white gouache, leaving the drips you like visible. (See E.)

5   If there are spaces between the bands of your rainbow, decide if you'd like to fill them with new colors or blend the edges of the existing colors. Make your colors as watery or bright as you like. There are many ways to paint a rainbow. (See F.)

Spiritual Focus, by Mary Rockwood Lane

The physiology of the relaxation and healing that result from deep emergence in creativity is similar to the physiology of prayer and meditation. Herbert Benson, M.D., of the Benson-Henry Institute at Harvard Medical School, first wrote about these effects in his classic book, *The Relaxation Response*, in 1975. He showed that meditation alone lowered blood pressure, heart rate, and breathing rate, and could be used as a primary therapy for heart disease patients. Today, Dean Ornish, M.D., founder of the Preventive Medicine Research Institute in Sausalito, California, uses meditation as part of his heart disease regimen, to reduce stress. He also uses it for its spiritual focus to reduce alienation and promote feelings of connectedness and oneness. The meditative state we achieve by making art is powerful because it involves all the senses at once. It helps to change brainwave states and deals with both the outer world and inner world.

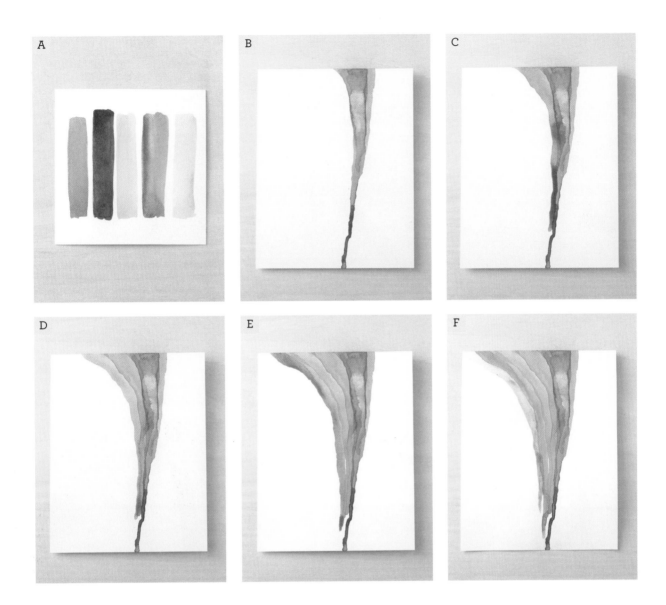

DRAWING CALM

HARMONIZING ON A LINE

The way a selection of notes comes together to form a perfect chord is undeniably pleasing. Kazimir Malevich formed a visual chord of modern music in this painting, with grace notes joining from the sides. We'll use his chord as inspiration for a collage filled with shapes and colors in space. There are myriad possibilities for combining the elements—and creating harmony. As you work, notice how adding one element makes you think about the shape, color, and placement of the next, similar to finding the right notes to combine as one. Keep an open mind as you play with the elements on your page. Enjoy the process, and consider listening to music as you work. Music helps things flow and adds a soundtrack to the process of making art.

YOU WILL NEED:

- sheets of mixed-media paper, any size
- gouache paints
- paintbrushes, in a variety of sizes
- scissors or a craft knife with a cutting surface
- 11" x 14" (28 x 35.5 cm) sheet of heavy watercolor paper
- white gesso for the background tone, optional
- matte medium
- colored pencils
- graphite pencil
- black Micron pens

Suprematist Composition No. 56, Kazimir Severinovich Malevich, Russian (1878–1935). Oil on canvas, 1936. State Russian Museum, St. Petersburg/ Bridgeman Images.

1   Plan your palette using three main colors with black as an accent. In addition, choose a brighter version of one of your main colors. If you've chosen a deep blue, for instance, pick a lighter, brighter blue as well. Paint each of five sheets of mixed-media paper with one of the colors and allow them to dry. (See A.)

2   Spread out the painted sheets and think about the shapes you'd like to work with. Cut out rectangles, strips, circles, and crescents. Make sure you have a few larger shapes along with smaller ones. There's no need to cut everything out all at once; you can allow for spontaneity later on in the process. At this point, just have enough to get started. (See B.)

3   Place the watercolor paper on your work surface. If the white background seems too bright, give it a light wash of color. Then, begin planning where you might place your shapes. In thinking about your composition, refer to the Malevich painting. Notice there's a strong line that extends diagonally from top left to bottom right. Most of the colored shapes fall along that line or spring from it. This line is a central chord that other notes play upon. (See C.)

4   Draw or visualize your line and begin to arrange your cut-out shapes. There's no need to fill every space—having some line exposed will help your composition. Shape by shape, build your composition, using matte medium to glue the pieces in place. Use tiny shapes and larger ones in a variety of colors. Keep the idea of harmony in mind. When you place one piece, are you moved to add another piece to balance it? If the elements look too balanced, add a fresh point for contrast. (See D and E.)

5   What about the space around the central chord? Try different shapes there to see how they interact with the core design. If you've been using all rectangles and strips, for instance, add a circle and a crescent to the mix. Add a pencil line to connect some of the shapes or doodle in the white space of the page. Play with the composition until you feel good about the balance of color, marks, and shapes. (See F.)

If you have leftover shapes and pieces, start a new collage. Try a smaller version, changing the angle of the line. Play and let the word "harmony" guide your choices.

A

B

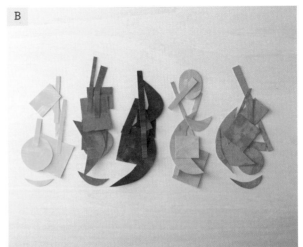

C

D

E

F

ONE CLOUD

Harmony is the perfect spring day. This painting by Arkhip Ivanovich Kuindzhi captures it with a rich blue sky, lush green grass, and a beautiful cloud directly in the center. The simplicity of the composition and the cleanness of the color palette feels relaxing and quiet. Use this painting as a reference for a collage, or find another cloud image that speaks to you.

YOU WILL NEED:

- 8″ x 10″ (20.5 cm x 25.5 cm) watercolor paper, canvas board, or primed panel

- pencil

- several pages from magazines or catalogs that have black type on a white page

- additional catalog pages with green and blue tones

- scissors

- gouache paints

- paintbrushes, in a variety of sizes

- craft glue or matte medium

- pencil or charcoal stick

A Small Cloud, Arkhip Ivanovich Kuindzhi, Russian (1842–1910). Oil on panel. Odessa Fine Arts Museum, Ukraine/Bridgeman Images.

1   Place a piece of watercolor paper horizontally on your work surface. With the pencil, lightly map out placement for your main elements. In the Kuindzhi painting, the grass fills about a quarter of the composition, leaving the rest for the sky. If you place your horizon line higher, you will have more grass and less sky and your cloud might interrupt both planes. Choose where you will be placing your cloud and roughly how large you want to make it. (See A.)

2   Organize the catalog or magazine pages. Pages with a white background will be used for the cloud. Those with a darker blue or green background will form the cloud's shadow. Note that black type on white paper can be lighter or darker, denser or airier. Cut shapes from the pages, keeping in mind the cloud shape you'd like to make. Rounder shapes cut in various sizes will eventually be collaged together to create a cloud with some varied lights and darks. Cut a pile of shapes to choose from. (See B.)

3   Paint your landscape in gouache, starting with the foreground. Create an expanse of lawn with lights and darks, using several shades of green. (See C.)

4   In painting the sky, the darkest shades of blue will appear at the top. The blues will become lighter, gradually turning into white as you approach the horizon. (See D.)

5   When the paint has dried, arrange the cut cloud pieces on the sky background. Begin gluing the pieces into place. Add the small pieces one by one, building the cloud. Pay attention to the density of the type on the pages. Does the cloud look too dark? Add some lighter pieces. (See E.)

6   Stand back to look at how your composition is coming together. Do you want to create a smaller cloud to balance the other? Build it the same way you did the first. (See F.)

7   Now create the shadow beneath your cloud. Apply cut pieces of blue or green paper on the grassy area in a shape that feels right. If you see other places where you'd like to create a little more texture, add more cut paper shapes to the surface. (See G.)

8   As a final step, pencil in lines or shading that help tie together the composition. Enjoy the process and reflect on other versions of this project you could create. Perhaps a series of three cloud collages with different color palettes, or different kinds of clouds?

A

B

C

D

E

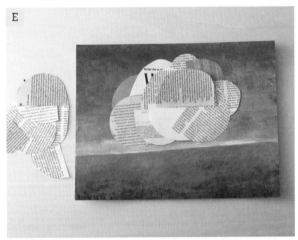

F

G

DRAWING CALM

OCEAN IMPRESSION

Monet's colorful painting has an energy to it while still allowing the viewer to experience the calming effects of the sea. His color palette and brushstrokes above and below the horizon convey the changing light on clouds and waves, as though he caught the passage of time in a single frame.

We'll use Monet's color palette to make a collage of tiny bits of torn paper. You can develop this project over a period of time. Collect the colored paper you want to use as you go along, tear it into small bits when the spirit moves you (so satisfying!), and glue the pieces into place when you're ready.

YOU WILL NEED:

- colored pencils, gouache paints, or watercolors

- scrap paper

- magazines and catalogs

- variety pack of colored construction paper

- 8″ x 10″ (20.5 x 25.5 cm) Bristol board

- matte medium or glue stick

- small paintbrush

- scissors or craft knife

- graphite pencil

On the High Seas, Sunset at Pourville; Coucher de Soleil a Pourville, Pleine Mer. Claude Monet, French (1840–1926). Oil on canvas, 1882. Private Collection/Bridgeman Images.

1   Using Monet's painting as a guide, create a color palette. It helps to have a color reference while you're looking for pages to tear from magazines and catalogs. Use colored pencils and a piece of scrap paper to jot down the range of pinks, yellows, blues, greens, and lavenders that you'd use. (See A.)

2   Look through your collection of magazines, catalogs, and construction paper. Find colors that relate to the palette you've made and tear out the pages. You may not find exactly what you are looking for, but be open to what you find. (You can also paint sheets of paper using the colors you want and allow them to dry.)

3   When you've gathered a pile of pages, tear them into pieces. Think about sizes and shapes, keeping in mind that you'll be mimicking the look of Monet's brushstrokes. In Monet's painting, the brushstrokes that create the sky are much longer than the strokes that make the water. Create piles of torn bits by color and size. Imperfect edges and varied sizes are fine to play with. Don't worry about matching anything exactly. (See B.)

4   Set the Bristol board horizontally on your work surface. Use a neutral color to paint the surface for the background. Allow it to dry and draw the horizon line. Look at Monet's painting, studying the way he dispersed color throughout. Notice where bright, pale yellow suggests sunlight in the sky and how the horizon line is made up of the darkest tones. (See C.)

5   Choose a few general areas of color on which to concentrate first—the blue just above the horizon in the sky perhaps, or the darkest areas of the ocean. For the sky, choose your longest strips of blue and apply them to the background with matte medium. For the sea, go with your darkest small pieces of paper. The variety in paper sizes alone will create enough contrast to separate the two areas. (See D.)

6   Keep adding pieces with matte medium to create the sea and sky. If you find you need transitional, neutral pieces between colors, go back to the magazines and pull out a few more pages.

7   When your seascape is just the way you like it, brush on a light coat of matte medium to seal it.

Do this project using any photographs or paintings you like as your reference guides. Create a loose interpretation of the image or get more precise and add tiny details. This project is a translation; each time you do it, it will be totally unique.

A

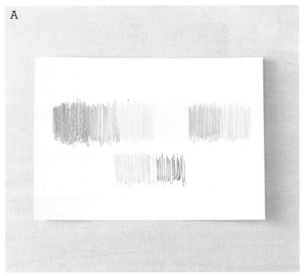

B

C

D

CHAPTER 6

CALM

It doesn't take long to notice when artwork has a calming effect. Some color palettes are naturally calming—think blues and grays. In addition, the repetition of marks, composition, subject matter, and other details of a painting impact whether or not it leaves the viewer with a sense of tranquility.

The works of art in this chapter share a similar peaceful feel. The compositions are quiet, the color palettes are tranquil in tone, and they feel organized and calm.

"Art washes from the soul the dust of everyday life."
—Pablo Picasso

◄ *The Iles d'Or (The Iles d'Hyeres*, Var).
Henri-Edmond Cross, French (1856–1910).
Oil on canvas, c. 1891–92. Musée d'Orsay, Paris/
Bridgeman Images.

STACKS OF CALM

The repetition and related colors that Paul Klee used in *Growth of the Night Plants* move your eye up and down through the stacks of shapes as they emerge from their nighttime background. Perhaps it's no surprise that Klee was an accomplished musician with a great feeling for rhythm. In this project, we'll create a collage using painted-paper shapes that we've cut out, echoing the shapes in the Klee painting. The organic movement of forms creates a balanced and peaceful composition.

YOU WILL NEED:

- 9″ x 12″ (23 x 30.5 cm) canvas board

- black and white gesso

- paintbrush

- sheets of watercolor or mixed-media paper, in a variety of sizes

- watercolor paint

- scissors or craft knife

- matte medium

- dry brush or sponge, optional

Growth of the Night Plants (no. 174). Paul Klee, Swiss (1879–1940). Oil on cardboard, 1922. Pinakothek der Moderne, Munich/ Bayerische Staatsgemäldesammlungen/ Artists Rights Society/Bridgeman Images.

1. Prepare the background. Paint the canvas board with black gesso. It doesn't matter if the color isn't perfectly uniform. I mixed in a bit of white gesso in places to give the black some variance. Allow the paint dry completely.

2. Decide how many colors you'd like in your palette. Use Klee's palette as a guide, or make your own. Consider including neutrals, as they are a quiet force. Experiment with different shades of the same color; your goal is to create color fields. Subtle differences, brushstrokes, and imperfections are all welcome—they will add character and interest. Using watercolor, paint one sheet of paper completely with each of your different colors. Allow the paint to dry completely. (See A.)

3. Decide on the range of shapes you'd like to have in your piece. You can stick to squares, triangles, circles (a little harder to cut!), or any combination of these in a variety of sizes and colors. Cut them out and sort them by shape. (See B.)

4. Set your painted background vertically on your workspace. Experiment with placing your cut-out shapes on the background, without gluing anything yet. Play with the stacks of colors and shapes until you find a design that pleases you. Refer to Klee's piece if you need a little more structure. (See C and D.)

5. Use the matte medium to glue the shapes into place, starting with the bottom of each pictorial stack. Brush medium on the first shape, place it where you'd like it, then brush medium over it. Repeat, adding each shape and brushing over it with more medium, until you reach the top shape of each stack. Allow the matte medium to dry completely. There will be a slight white cast to the brushed medium, but it will dry clear. (See E.)

6. Once the piece is dry, decide if there is anything you want to add to it. Do you have leftover shapes? Do you want to cut out smaller ones and add those?

7. You may wish to use a sponge or dry brush and a tiny dab of white gesso to highlight the top of some of the shapes. Similarly, you can add shadows with the black gesso.

Are you happy with the colors you chose? Do you want to try different shapes? Think about ways you'd like to play with color and shape and try the project again. Enjoy every step of the way. Focus on each step as you go, settle in, relax, and lose track of time!

A DELICATE CALM

Plants and flowers provide great subject matter for exploring a medium and loosening up in a sketchbook. (They are very patient, nonjudgmental models!) One of the things I love about this watercolor drawing is that Charles Rennie Mackintosh had such a light touch. It feels as if he relaxed in making this sketch, and enjoyed the shapes, colors, and gentle lines. What could be more calming?

For this project, we'll use watercolor and pencils. For inspiration, use any plant you like, real or imagined. I chose poppies. We'll take a playful approach—explore, doodle, drip. No heavy paint here, just interesting pencil lines and drips of color.

YOU WILL NEED:

- paper or sketchbook, any size
- graphite pencil
- colored pencils
- sheets of watercolor paper, 9″ x 12″ (23 x 30.5 cm)
- watercolor paints
- paintbrushes, in a variety of sizes
- black Micron pen

Cactus Flower. **Charles Rennie Mackintosh, Scottish (1868–1928). Watercolor on paper, 1915. Sheffield Galleries and Museums Trust, UK/ Museums Sheffield/Bridgeman Images.**

1   Look at the plant or picture you've chosen as your model, and explore it as though it's the first time you've ever looked at a plant. Look at the colors, the shapes, the way the leaves attach to the stem, the weight of the flowers, and the way all the different parts of the plant fit together.

2   Now try making a doodle of your plant with pencil on paper. Don't be intimidated—it's a casual doodle and you're just exploring. Play with your pencil lines, experimenting with deep, light, and varied pressure. See what each quality of line evokes; your line can describe what you are drawing. (See A.)

3   What stands out to you in your doodle? Are there parts of it that you love? Use your doodle as the basis for a new drawing on the watercolor paper. Continue to improvise, discover, and play as you draw. There's no need to draw a single, realistic plant—if you'd like, make a dreamy assemblage of flowers and leaves.

4   When you've loosely sketched your plant, look at it to see which parts pique your curiosity. Go back into the drawing and, with a more confident line, add emphasis or a sense of playfulness. (See B.)

5   Look at the drawing again. Are there areas where you'd like to add light watercolor? Mix the watercolor tones you prefer and let the color drip off the brush into areas of your drawing, allowing the color and the dripped quality to remain spontaneous. (See C.)

6   When the paint dries, go back in and deepen some of the pencil lines or use black pen to do the same. Add patterns or details to the flowers or background. If colored pencils appeal to you, use them to work in a little more definition or simply add color. (See D.)

Take a look at your painted sketch to see if there's anything else you'd like to add before moving on. Does your painting speak quietly or shout emphatically? If you've made a quiet drawing, you might try a louder one—or vice versa. Try this exercise with another plant, keeping it light—explore, doodle, drip. This exercise is a great way to focus on something and get in touch with details that speak to you.

A

B

C

D

SEVEN SHAPES

In this collage, Olga Rozanova used seven pieces of paper, each one a different color. Yet they all combine happily on the blue background, complementing one another nicely. There's nothing fussy, overworked, or too detailed in her collage. This project offers an opportunity to play with different colors, patterns, and shapes on a colored background. It's a simple exercise, and yet, finding a perfect balance of shapes can be immensely calming.

YOU WILL NEED:

- magazine or discarded book

- sheets of colored paper, construction paper, origami paper, or other patterned paper, any size

- sturdy piece of paper for your surface, preferably not white, 9″ x 12″ (23 x 30.5 cm)

- gouache paints and paintbrush, optional

- scissors and/or craft knife

- cutting surface

- glue stick

Fight Against the Ocean. Olga Vladimirovna Rozanova, Russian (1886–1918). Collage, 1916. Tretyakov Gallery, Moscow/Bridgeman Images.

1 Cut a few pages from a magazine or book, preferably some with words and some with illustration. Add these to the other colored papers that you've assembled. Of the assortment you've gathered, choose seven with which to work. Consider your background color when deciding which papers to use. Feel free to paint any of the papers to add variety. (See A.)

2 Think about the shapes you want to work with and cut them out. Choose one shape that will be the focal point of your composition. You can use basic shapes, including circles, ovals, rectangles, or abstract shapes that suggest a flower, a face, or anything else. You might also cut a few different smaller versions of each shape. (See B.)

3 Place the shapes on the background sheet and play with them. Allow some to overlap and think about how the shapes float or live in the space around them. When you've reached a balance that you like, glue the pieces into place.

Do you like the way the text, patterns, and colors work on the background? Make another collage, altering the background color and paper shapes. Pay special attention to the background and give your paper shapes room to breathe.

Communicate and Connect, by Mary Rockwood Lane
The time we set aside to create and make art has powerful healing benefits. It allows us to tap into our interior healing resources that shift us from the state of stress to the state of calmness. The benefit of calm and inner peace is a shift in our physiological state. Research supports that these benefits include a decrease in illness episodes, better sleep, and an enhanced immune system. There are many psychological benefits as well. The art experience increases our ability to communicate and connect with each other—it's a reflective process that can deepen our own understanding of ourselves.

A

B

IMAGINARY LANDSCAPE

Henri-Edmond Cross combined three things to give his painting a deeply relaxing sense of calm: an ocean vista, soft color, and pointillist patterns. The layers of color draw your eye back as far as the horizon with no interruption. Ah!

In this project, we'll create a fictitious landscape in acrylic. We'll use Cross's pointillism as inspiration for technique, but make our own composition and color palettes.

YOU WILL NEED:

- sheets of scrap paper
- pencils
- primed panel, canvas board, or heavy paper, 8″ x 10″ (20 x 25.5 cm)
- acrylic paints

- palette or ceramic plate
- round items in different sizes and diameters for making marks: the end of a wood dowel, the eraser of a pencil, your fingertip, or anything else that will make a dot shape

The Iles d'Or (The Iles d'Hyeres, Var).
Henri-Edmond Cross, French (1856–1910).
Oil on canvas, c. 1891–92. Musée d'Orsay,
Paris/Bridgeman Images.

1   Think about your fantasy landscape—what do you like to gaze at? Water, sand, and sky? Mountains and valleys? Grassy meadows? Make a sketch of your ideal vista on scrap paper. (See A.)

2   Think about your color palette. You might choose the colors of a sunset, the dawn, or a field of wildflowers. Choose the colors for each area of your landscape. (See B.)

3   Set out your background panel and sketch the outlines of your landscape. Squeeze some paint and mix one of the lighter colors for your painting. Pick up the dowel, load the end with paint, and cover your panel with dots of color. Allow the paint to dry. (See C and D.)

4   Mix the color for the foreground. Load your dowel, and begin making small dots, side by side and across the page. You can make them slowly and meditatively, or you can work quickly and more randomly. Leave tiny bits of background color peeking through the dots. Allow the color to dry. (See E.)

5   Now work on the middle ground of your painting. If you have differently sized dot-making tools, experiment with how they affect your painting. Continue to add band after band of color. Do the same with the sky or background of your painting, so that all the layers of the landscape are roughly painted. (See E and F.)

6   Notice in Henri Cross's painting how the bands of color used for the sand, sea, and sky are each made up of more than one color. Starting back at the bottom of your painting, add new dots of color that help describe each area. Mix in a few contrasting or alternate colors. (See G.)

7   Look at the transitions between each band of color. They will look more natural if they're somewhat uneven. Allow some of dots of color to rise above or fall below the transition line.

8   Add nuances to complete your imaginary vista. Deeper tones may help define certain areas, making them recede or pop.

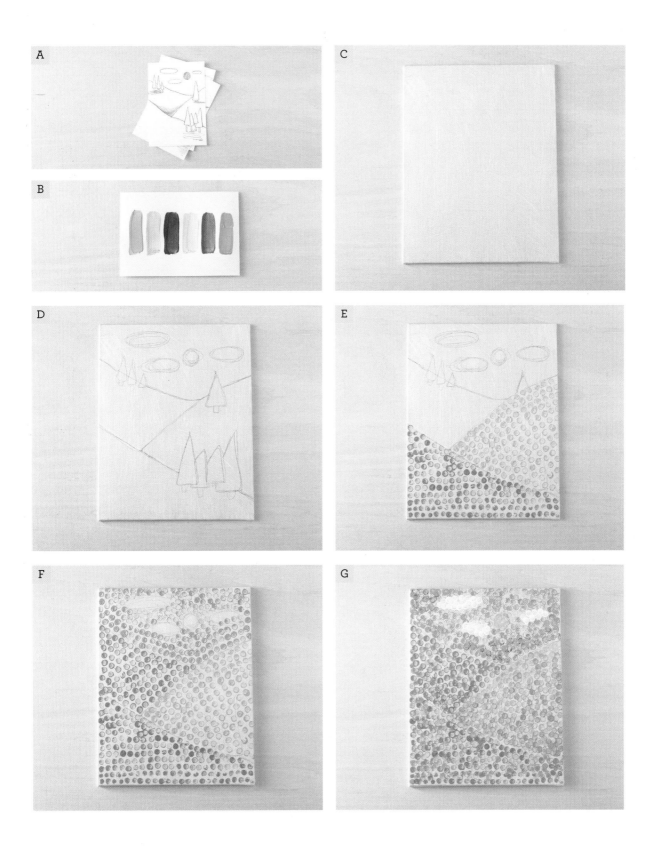

CHAPTER 7

LIGHT

In nature, photography, paintings, and in other works of art, we find beauty in the way we see light. It has the power to lift, awe, and delight. Whether an artist crafts beautiful effects that mimic light in nature or a photographer captures other-worldly light against a series of buildings, light creates a wonderful and magical focus. The quality of light can set the mood of a painting in an instant. Whether light is warmed by the sun, cooled by the moon, dappled by trees, or bright with a shock of saturated color, note how light speaks to you in a painting. With the projects in this section, think about how the light affects the tone or mood of your work.

◄ *Woodland Scene; Sous-bois*. Paul Cézanne, French (1839–1906). Watercolor over pencil on paper, c. 1900–1904. Private Collection/ Bridgeman Images.

DRAWING CALM

LINEAR SUNSET/PINK SKY (COLLAGE)

PROJECT 1

Monet caught a soft glowing light in this painting. It's a loose, sketchy landscape, yet it captures a familiar moment of awe at nature's colors. It's also a reminder that light can be pink, orange, and many tones of blue. For this project we'll use Monet's color palette to create a collage of painted paper.

YOU WILL NEED:

- acrylics or gouache paints
- paintbrushes, in a variety of sizes
- six small pieces of mixed-media or watercolor paper
- pencil

- scrap paper
- craft knife or scissors
- Bristol board or heavy paper, any size
- matte medium

Sunset at Lavacourt, 1880, Claude Monet (1840–1926). Oil on canvas. Private Collection/Bridgeman Images.

1   Start by looking at Monet's sunset. Notice the pink in the sky and how it sets the mood for the entire painting. It creates the bright spots of interest in the sea of neutrals and gray-blues. Think about the palette you want to use. We're looking for six colors, or ranges of color, for this project: pink, light blue, darker gray-blue, gray, and a warm neutral.

2   Paint each of the six pieces of paper. Use the colors you selected in step 1, but vary them as a range of shades when you paint them. Take this step slowly and enjoy the process of painting the gradations on each page; it can be very meditative and relaxing. Allow the paint to dry completely. (See A.)

3   Paint the sheet of Bristol board a neutral gray, or gray with a bit of blue. While the background tone dries, think about how you might compose your collage and make sketches of the layout. (See B.)

4   Cut the six small pieces of painted paper into horizontal strips of varying widths. Leave a few larger pieces for any improvised cutting you want do when you put your collage together. (See C.)

5   Place the Bristol board horizontally on your work surface, and imagine the sunset you want to create. You'll add the sun later, but decide where you want it to be. Add strips for the sky surrounding the sun area. Trim the strips shorter if you need to. Overlap the strips to be visually appealing as you lay them down. Arrange them roughly at first. Once you have planned the general layout, use the matte medium to adhere the strips to the surface. Work in small sections at a time. You'll start to see the sunset scene fill in. Notice how the neutral strips make the brighter colors pop.

6   Paint and cut the sun from an extra piece of paper, or draw and paint it on the collaged page. (See D.)

7   Look at your composition and note whether there are places that need additional matte medium, more color, or touches of black or white. (See E.)

Do you feel the sunset? Does the pink create a similar warm mood as it does in the Monet painting? You can repeat this exercise with different colors or as a nightscape with the moon instead of the sun. Play with light and notice which colors lend themselves to a sunny scene versus a cooler night scene. Play with season and how color relates to summer or autumn, or any other scene you'd like to explore. Enjoy being the master of your own light. What light feels the most calming or peaceful to you? You can use your color discoveries with more versions of this project, in addition to any other art making or doodling you may do.

A

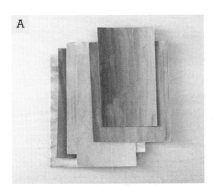

B

C

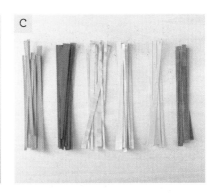

D

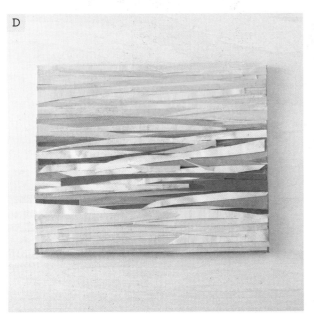

E

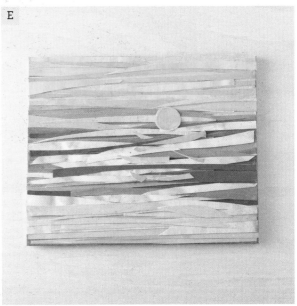

DRAWING CALM

NIGHTTIME TREESCAPE

There is a little bit of magic to be seen in a sky lit by the moon and stars, or streetlights lighting a path, or fireflies dotting a dark backyard on a summer night. The quality of light that each of these scenarios produces along with the surroundings that are gently illuminated, can create a scene of mystery and curiosity. Night scenes have a sense of calm and stillness to them as well. In this project, we'll create our own night scene, inspired by *A Park at Night*, by Jozsef Rippl-Ronai.

YOU WILL NEED:

- acrylic, gouache, or chalkboard paint
- paintbrushes, in a variety of sizes
- canvas board or sturdy paper that can handle wet media, 9" x 12" (23 x 30 cm)
- scrap paper or a sketchbook to work out the composition

- pencil
- black pastel or charcoal
- blending stick, optional
- scrap paper for testing limited color palette
- white pastel

A Park at Night, Jozsef Rippl-Ronai, Hungarian (1861–1927). Pastel on canvas, c. 1892–95. Musée d'Orsay, Paris/Bridgeman Images.

1. Prepare your painting surface. Mix a little white and blue into black paint, so it is a deep blue-gray. Paint the canvas board edge to edge. Once it's dry, brush a very thin, warm-white wash over the page. Ensure the color still reads as a rich gray. Allow it to dry. (See A.)

2. Draw a few trees on the sketchpad. We'll keep the design simple with a group of five trees. You can make graphic trees with round tops, traditional trees with full, leafy tops, or any other types of trees you are drawn to. Because this is a night scene, the shapes of the trees are much more important than any tiny details. (See B.)

3. Using a pencil or white pastel, sketch the trees onto the night surface. Arrange the bases of the trees at different levels to allow for the foreground's grassy surface. Place the trees so that they appear to grow at intervals between the foreground and mid ground.

4. Paint the trees with gouache or chalkboard paint that is close in tone to the background. There should be some contrast, but not a lot. Use the same color to paint the grassy area. Allow the paint to dry. (See C.)

5. Go into the background above the horizon line with the black pastel and add more depth to the gray. Smudge it into the background. (See D.)

6. Go back over the trees and grass with a lighter color than you used in the first round: A touch of a contrasting color will pop against the dark surface. It shouldn't be high contrast in a night scene; the entire palette in this painting is very subtle, which adds to the mood. (See E.)

7. Using the black pastel or charcoal, add additional depth to the middle section, between the trees. Use your finger or a blending stick to blend in the color.

8. Add other details, like stars, a moon, or a light post near the trees. Imagine the impact that the light will have. Does the moon cast a glow on some of the treetops? Perhaps the stars are just tiny lights in the field of the dark sky. Refine your painting any way you'd like, and let it dry. (See F.)

Enjoy how minimal a night painting can be, and how quiet and calm it can feel without the suggestion of bright sunlight or endless details to focus on. Create additional night paintings with houses, mountains, or any element you'd like. The possibilities are endless.

A

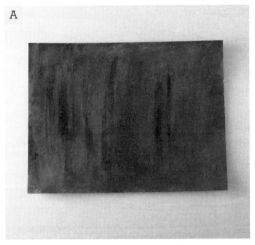

B

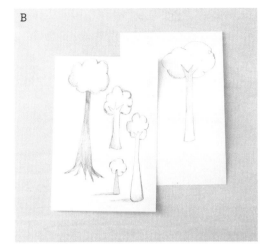

C

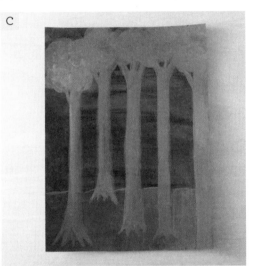

D

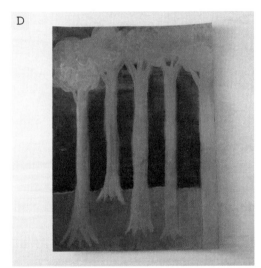

E

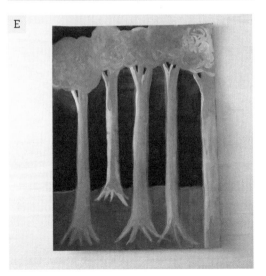

F

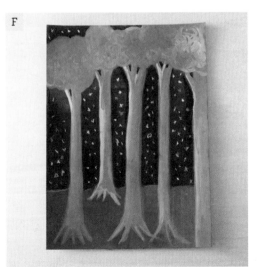

GOLD LEAF LIGHT

This project is a meditation on light and volume. There is a sea of whiteness, so you will be finding subtle ways to create texture and mass with paint, while letting gold leaf enter in as the brightest spot on the page. Stay open to the process, and don't worry about the finished painting looking any particular way. This is an exploration with paint and gold leaf—how you bring them together is up to you.

YOU WILL NEED:

- scrap paper or sketchbook, any size
- pencil
- small stretched canvas or canvas board
- acrylic paints
- paintbrushes, in a variety of sizes
- gold leaf
- glue or matte medium for gold leaf

TOP: *Sandviken, Norway*. Claude Monet, French (1840–1926). Oil on canvas, 1895. Private Collection/Bridgeman Images.

BOTTOM: *Sky Study*. Joseph Mallord William Turner, British (1775–1851). Watercolor on paper, c. 1845. Private Collection/Agnew's, London/Bridgeman Images.

1   Sketch a loose composition on your scrap paper. You can create a cloudscape with no reference to land or a mountaintop with clouds above it. Work with an odd number of clouds. (See A.)

2   Once you have a rough plan, sketch it on your canvas. (See B.)

3   We'll keep our palette very white and light, using only hints of other colors. Plan out a rough color palette that appeals to you. Light pinks, golds, and blues will create a limited but beautiful palette with the overall white. Consider the gold leaf as a color, too.

    Think about mood when choosing colors. You can tell a different story, depending on the colors you use. A soft, neutral palette might feel quiet, while various blues might feel cool and calm. Experiment with colors that feel as if they fit with the painting you want to make. (See C.)

4   Start by painting a textural surface. Using white as your base, add the supporting colors lightly throughout. Create a surface with texture and varied tones. Let it dry before moving on. (See D.)

5   Start adding the compositional elements. In making a cloudscape, you can alternate between white and your supporting colors to create interest and volume. Adding shadow will provide depth and weight. Brighter spots will help the clouds pop from the background. Move intuitively across your page, painting in the clouds and mountains, if you have them. Allow the paint to dry. (See E.)

6   Think about where you'd like to add the gold leaf. It could be the sun peeking over the mountain, a thin gold line edging the mountaintops, or a flash of light coming from behind a cloud or off in the distance. This will create a point of contrast and light that cuts through your very white painting.

7   Apply the glue where you'd like to add the gold. Carefully add the gold leaf and let the glue dry completely. After it dries, carefully brush away any excess gold leaf with a soft, dry brush or cloth. (See F.)

8   Now that you see the impact the gold light is having, decide on what kinds of refinements you'd like to make. You can work organically, going back and forth between adding tone to your clouds and background and adding or painting over some of the gold leaf.

When the painting is dry, you can go back in and add pencil line if you like. These can be loose lines that help to describe your clouds or that add definition. It's completely up to you.

Note on gold leaf: You can purchase imitation or composite gold leaf at most craft stores. It comes in very thin sheets, often separated by pieces of tissue paper. Store it safely until you're ready to use it. Tweezers may be helpful for moving it from the packaging to your surface.

Gold leaf flakes very easily, which you can use to your advantage as you adhere it to your painting. It takes some practice to work with, but after playing with it a bit, you'll see the possibilities for using it in any art project you can dream up.

Light to the Darkness, by Mary Rockwood Lane

The connection between creating art and feeling physical and psychological benefits from it is simple and natural. In our imagination, we bring light to the darkness blocking us. In the process, we see images that we can extract and bring outward into the light of day in the form of art. The creative process affects our immune system, our blood flow, our attitudes—it's a vital element in our health.

CHAPTER 8

·················

RHYTHM

There's a reason we listen to music to relax. Rhythms lift us and carry us with them. In art, symmetry and pattern are visual rhythms, and, like music, can do wonders for a busy mind. Shapes repeated, symmetrical, or simply ordered, rest the eyes and spirit. Through repeated objects, negative space, and use of color, you can create your own visual "music."

Patterns are everywhere in paintings and the decorative arts. You'll find patterns in borders, in fabrics, quilts, wallpapers, and every other surface that can be decorated. They can be quiet and sparse, meticulously organized, or feel more like a random collection of images. We'll play with pattern in this chapter. Enjoy the peacefulness that comes from making an ordered system, and throw a little whimsy in to shake things up. Let the framework of symmetry and pattern help you find a little calm in your day.

◄ *Willow Bough*, William Morris, British (1834–1896). Color woodcut on paper, c. 1900. Art Gallery of South Australia, Adelaide/Bridgeman Images.

DRAWING CALM

PATTERNED RIBBONS

This Mexican sampler includes more than a dozen different patterns, but because they're stacked as narrow ribbons and similar colors repeat throughout the stack, they harmonize beautifully. This antique sampler is embroidered. We'll make our patterned ribbons with paper and paint.

YOU WILL NEED:

- black Micron pens

- scrap paper or sketchbook

- six sheets of mixed-media paper, cut to 6″ x 8″ (15 x 20 cm)

- acrylic paints

- paintbrush

- scissors or craft knife

- white Gelly Roll pen

- 8″ x 10″ (20 x 25.5 cm) card stock or cardboard

- matte medium or glue

Embroidery Sampler, Mexican School. Cotton, nineteenth century. Private Collection/ Bridgeman Images.

1. Make doodles on the scrap paper, any way that appeals. Create several pages of shapes, lines, and designs with no particular agenda. Take as much time as you need. (See A.)

2. Once you have a few pages of doodles, look at the shapes and designs you've created. Pick out several that you like and imagine them in repeat patterns. We'll be making six ribbon patterns that will sit next to one another.

3. Brush thinned acrylic paint over sheets of mixed-media paper. Keep it simple by using just a few calm colors, such as blue or gray, or a single color to cover the page. Allow the paint to dry. (See B.)

4. Cut the painted paper into strips 8″ (20 cm) long, but of varied widths. (Cut more than six if you'd like to have options when you work out your patterns.) (See C.)

5. Pick one of your doodled designs and choose one of the painted strips. Use a Micron pen or the white Gelly Roll pen to draw your designs on the strip, as ordered or as random as you like. Continue filling in your pattern strip by strip. (See D.)

6. Add additional colors or details to your patterns. Maybe color every other circle blue or the smallest shape on each strip red. Consider the color within each strip, as well as within your group of strips. (See E.)

7. Choose six or more strips to mount on the card stock. Arrange them on the background and play with how they sit next to one another. Decide what color you'd like to make the background. Paint the card stock and allow it to dry completely. (See F.)

8. Glue the pattern strips in place. They can be glued edge to edge or with strips of the background between them. (See G.)

9. When the glue has dried, fine-tune the colors and repeat designs in your ribbons to create a pleasing rhythm. The next time you do this project, try a different rhythm.

Inner Artist, Inner Healer, by Mary Rockwood Lane

Each of us has an inner artist and an inner healer. The inner artist is the part that is passionately creative, falls in love, feels connected, is at home with who he or she is, but is also willing to explore. The inner healer is the part of us that balances the body, keeps us growing, and, more importantly, helps us recover when we're ill. By constantly reaffirming our strengths, energies, goals, and creativity, the inner artist helps release the inner healer when we need it most. You can use art to heal yourself, others, some aspect of your community, or the Earth!

A

B

C

D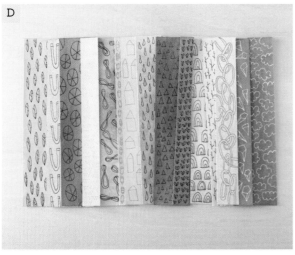

E

F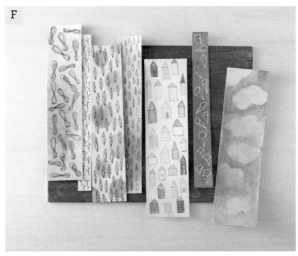

G

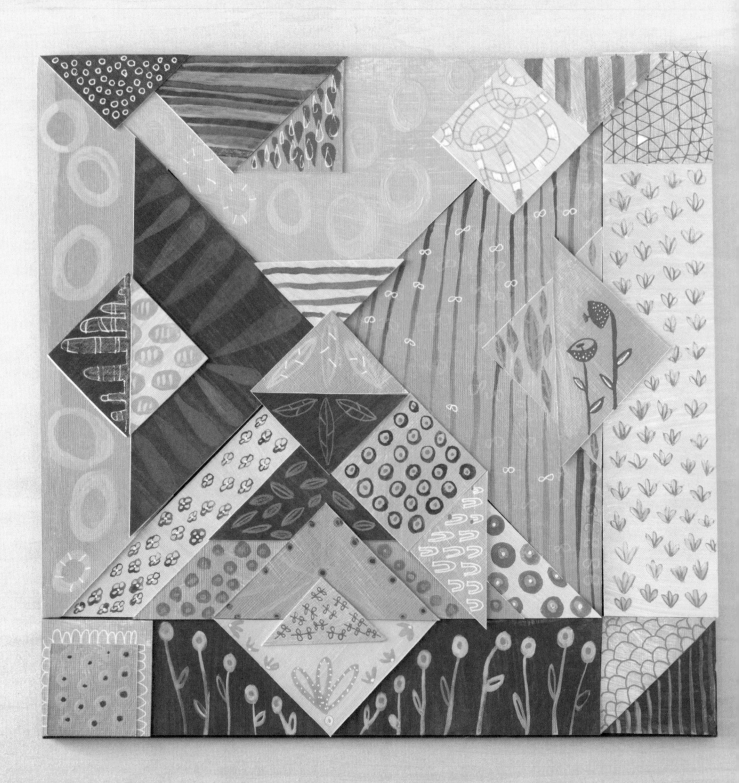

DRAWING CALM

DOODLE QUILT

The look of antique quilts gives such a feeling of comfort. In this project, we'll capture the look of an old quilt with cut paper. What's fun about a crazy quilt collage is that you can create vibrant patterns of color without worrying about the exact measurements and straight lines. In a crazy quilt, every piece can reflect a little bit of you.

YOU WILL NEED:

- scrap paper or sketchbook

- 4 or 5 pieces of 12″ x 12″ (30 x 30 cm) paper to use for painting and collage

- scissors or craft knife

- acrylic or gouache paints

- paintbrushes, in a variety of sizes

- black Micron pens

- white Gelly Roll pen

- piece of square card stock or cardboard, such as 10″ x 10″ (25 x 25 cm), for mounting the painted paper

- glue or double-sided adhesive for attaching shapes

- colored pencils, optional

Embroidered Crazy Patchwork Coverlet, English School. Velvet, silk, and wool, 1886. Quilt Museum and Gallery, York, UK/ Bridgeman Images.

1   Prepare the base for your collaged quilt with the card stock. Depending on how dense your collage will be, some of the card stock surface might show through. Choose whether to paint it black, a neutral color, or another tone. (See A.)

2   Choose your color palette and paint individual sheets of paper with those colors. A good balance might include a neutral or two, with two brighter colors. You can always add more color later. I chose black for my background, a gray, a tan, and two blues for my paper colors. Allow the paint to dry completely. (See B.)

3   Before cutting the painted paper into your quilting pieces, think about how you'd like the shapes to fit together. You can cut pieces to fit exactly within your square, or you can improvise as you go. Either approach is fine. Cut about half of each painted sheet into shapes. Keep your shapes simple and don't make them too small. (See C.)

4   Prepare your painted square surface with an adhesive. You can use glue or double-sided adhesive tape to align the edges. (See D.)

5   Start piecing in your shapes. (Don't press down on them firmly until you are sure of your placement.) You can start in the center, or at a corner and add shapes bit by bit. If you need to cut specific sizes, use the larger uncut pieces to fill in the gaps. Note how your color composition is coming together. Move pieces around until you're happy with your square. Press down firmly to adhere your shapes. (See E.)

6   Now for the details. You can approach this step with paint, colored pencils, or both. Take each shape into consideration, and create a little world within each one. Do you want to make a circle pattern? Stripes? Maybe you want to make a doodle of a leaf or an acorn. Let each shape be its own little space, and let each space relate to the whole. Pay attention to how your drawings are oriented. You may not want everything facing the same way.

7   In the example quilt, you can see how the stitching serves as another pattern element. Feel free to add lines as if you are joining your pieces together. Get a little lost in your quilt, and add as many details as you'd like. If you've enjoyed the process, begin again, creating a new collage of shapes to draw upon. You can get a little more complex with your next one, or keep things simple and focus on the details inside the shapes. Quilting has a rich history and there is much inspiration to be found in it.

A
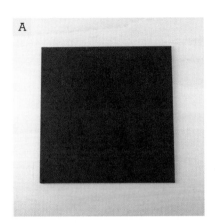

B
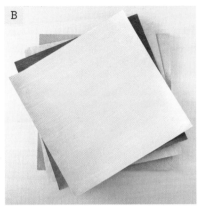

C
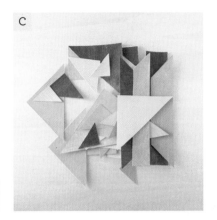

D
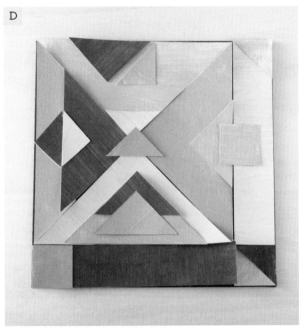

E

POLYPHONY

This project is an exploration of color, pattern, and texture. We will be rolling paint onto a surface as well as painting shapes and patterns with stencils. Klee's painting, *Polyphony* is a lovely piece with which to spend some time. Notice the implied order of squares or straight edges, as well as the repeating dot texture throughout. Notice his color choices and how juxtaposing certain colors can help the texture to recede or come to life. Refer to Klee's painting as you compose your own piece. As you work, notice how the elements sit together and how changing something minor can give your composition visual interest.

YOU WILL NEED:

- newsprint
- acrylic paints
- pencil or pen
- sketchpad or paper, any size
- small pieces of card stock, including scraps to use with the brayer
- scissors or craft knife
- sturdy pieces of cardboard or mat board for rolling out the paint

- brayer or paint roller
- scrap paper
- 9" x 12" (23 x 30.5 cm) Bristol board or primed wood panel
- small pieces of mesh or screen, or a stencil
- hole punch
- sponge or stipple brush

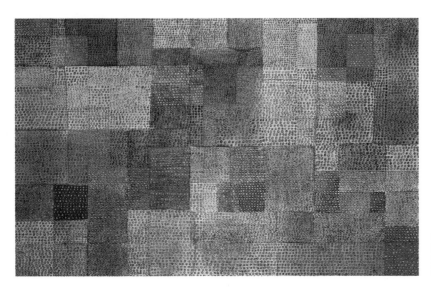

Polyphony, Paul Klee, Swiss (1879–1940). Tempera, 1932. M. Carrieri/Artists Rights Society/ Bridgeman Images.

1   Cover your work surface with newsprint. Choose five colors to create your palette. Choose neutral colors or white to contrast with brighter tones. Roll the paint onto a 9″ x 12″ (23 x 30.5 cm) panel. (See A.)

2   Draw some shapes in the sketchbook. Choose one shape to repeat in your composition—perhaps a cloud, house, leaf, blades of grass, or even squares or circles. Doodle on the paper until you settle on a main shape and draw it in three different sizes on a piece of card stock. Think small, but not too small. Cut out the shapes, creating stencils for your painting. Set them aside. (See B.)

3   Squeeze a dab of neutral color onto the cardboard. Roll the brayer through it to load it. Test the paint on scrap paper and then roll it on the Bristol board, making straight lines. Use scraps of card stock to help you create parallel lines in the paint. Let the paint dry a little before moving on to the next color. (See C.)

4   Rinse the brayer and roll out a new color. Use the cardboard scraps to help roll out strips, boxes, and rectangles of color on top of the first layer of color. Allow the paint to dry completely. If any of the colors become muddy, wait until the paint is completely dry before touching them up with fresh color. (See D and E.)

5   The next layer focuses on texture created with a stencil. You can purchase a stencil or make your own. I used two: one was a small piece of window screen and the other I made by punching many holes in a piece of card stock with a hole punch. (The screen allows painting to be applied in an ordered pattern.)

Note: Create or purchase a few versions of your stencils, so you can use one for each color and avoid accidently mixing them.

6   Set the painted Bristol board horizontally on your work surface. Decide where you would like to add texture and think about what color you'd like to use. Using a complementary color that is either lighter or darker than the background makes the texture appear to lift off the page. Place the stencil on the section you've chosen, dip the sponge into a small amount of paint, and gently stipple it over the stencil. Move the stencil to the next area and continue adding texture until you are satisfied. Allow the paint to dry completely. (See F.)

7   Now we'll use the shape stencil that you made in step 2. Look over your painting and see where you might want to add the shape(s). If you made leaves, do you want them cascading across the page? Do you want a very regimented row of circles that vary in size?

8   Decide where to position the main stencil on your painted board. Choose a paint color that contrasts with the background, dip the sponge in the paint, and gently stipple it over the stencil. Carefully remove the stencil and allow the paint to dry before adding another stenciled shape. You may change colors while repeating the same size and shape, or keep them the same and change stencil sizes. Take your time and find the balance in your composition, taking care to have something a little off or imperfect. (See G.)

9   If you want to fine-tune any stenciled areas with a brush, this is the time to do it.

A

B

C

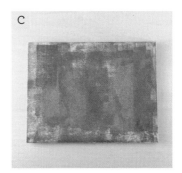

D

E

F

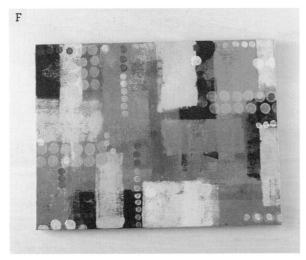

G

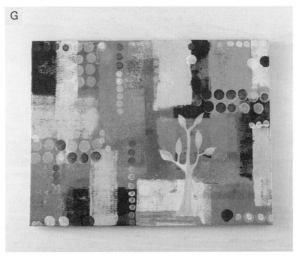

CHAPTER 9

MAINTAINING THE CALM

Sometimes I notice my creative mind is gathering information, and other times I'm drawn to making things. It isn't a hard boundary between the two states: it's easy to go back and forth from one to the other. When I'm not drawing or painting, often I'm reading, writing, flipping through magazines, looking at artist websites, or visiting galleries or museums. Allowing your preferences guide you is a good way to get inspired. If you're struggling with an art project, know when to walk away and give it some air. Come back to it when you're feeling refreshed and inspired. Uncover the layers of your creativity like quiet discoveries, and be grateful for the information and your awareness of it. In this chapter, we will walk through a few ways you can keep your creative mind flowing, whether or not you're actively creating art.

BE STILL, GO WITHIN

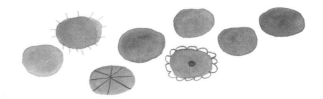

Sometimes creativity isn't about seeking inspiration, but reconnecting with yourself. There are countless ways to do this, but mindfulness meditation is a wonderful tool to have with you always. It helps you tune in, clear your mind, and quiet your internal chatter. To get started with meditation, seek out classes in your area, find a great book, or go online. A body scan meditation can be the perfect way to shift gears before settling in to work on a project. Bring mindfulness to your art making, as well as to every other aspect of your world. It doesn't require anything except you, your body, and your breath.

Finding Your Visual Cues

There are many ways to cultivate inspiration. Sometimes I go in waves of gathering inspiration and not producing much art. Other times, I'm in a heavy production mode when I'm not taking in too much from the outside. There are also times when I let the inspiration flow in, and let the work flow out. That is often when I feel the best about my work, as well as just about everything else. It's kind of a creative homeostasis.

We're surrounded by stimulation and visuals. If you live in an urban environment, your visuals are varied and quick. For those in a more rural setting, the visuals are also constant, but perhaps with a bit more air around them. Try not to resist what is in your world, and just take note.

Your Immediate Surroundings

What do you collect or hold on to? What objects have been passed down to you that hold stories? The paint colors you choose for your rooms, the artwork on your walls, and the knickknacks on your shelves—all of these details can inform you. Do you want to tell stories visually that have something to do with the items that make up your home? Or do you want to look elsewhere?

The Rabbit Hole (Internet)

The internet is an obvious influence. I regard it as a valuable tool for researching art and artists, as well as for online learning and cataloging things that I want to go back to.

One word of caution: it can be very easy to get lost researching. Time flies, and suddenly you've researched away your entire afternoon. I would suggest setting time limits on this kind of research, taking time to step away from the computer to research inspiration in person, or to actually get to working on a project.

You can find paced classes to do at your leisure, which can be a great way to expand your skills, and potentially get feedback on your work. There are also communities of students and teachers that are so helpful for both and inspiration and support. You don't have to look far to find a class or even a brief tutorial in just about any kind of art making imaginable.

Art Museums and Galleries

Perhaps you have an art museum, a natural history museum, and galleries available to you where you live. Pay a visit, wander around, bring a sketchbook, spend some time, and notice what resonates with you. Is there a color palette you can't get out of your head or a huge sculpture that reminds you of something? Let all of it pass through your filter, and see what stays with you.

Go Outside

A walk in my backyard can get me centered and focused within moments. My four-year-old daughter likes to pet the trees, and we both pick up rocks and sticks. Sometimes there is a heron that stands in the shallow water in the river behind our house and just stares at us silently. None of these details specifically informs my art making or my ability to relax or get quiet, but all of it does. The way the light hits the house or the cluster of trees nearby, the sound of kids playing a few yards over, all of it. Simply tuning in to our surroundings and becoming aware of what is going on around us can quiet our busy minds. If there are stones or sticks that you would like to have in your workspace or reading space, bring the outside in. I have little rocks from many different journeys over the years, and they just feel good to have around.

Art Books

Sometimes if I feel a bit stuck, I'll head to my bookshelves. I never know what I'm looking for, whether it's in a book of Francesco Clemente watercolors, a vintage book of typography, or a graphic novel by Chris Ware. It isn't anything I can put my finger on, but I always know when I've found it. I recommend having at least a few books that you can go to when you need to. Finding books in used bookshops can feel like the best treasure hunt ever.

Thrift Shops, Estate Sales, Garage Sales

If you are looking for a little inspiration, a visit to your local thrift shop or flea market can provide you with great, quirky things to discover. Whether you enjoy poking through the artwork, books, or ceramics, it's easy to get lost among treasures that may snap you out of a creative rut.

These are just a few ideas for how to jump-start your creativity by seeking out the things that you ultimately love to look at. It is a little like curating. Be curious and open, and recognize what strikes you: much of what is out in the world won't resonate in that way. Get to know your own tastes and preferences, and honor them. Not only will these gestures create a happy calm, but they can be the jumping off points for many stories, drawings, or paintings that you have yet to begin.

ADDITIONAL EXERCISES

Here are a few additional exercises that may help loosen you up and get things moving creatively. Turn to these exercises for a little recharge, or one-offs when you want to change gears, relax, and play—feel free to improvise! All of these exercises allow you to use your brain a bit differently than you usually do during the course of a normal day. There are elements of composition, creative problem-solving, and even color palette decisions at play here—stay open and see where they take you.

Draw Your Walk

Something as basic as walking outdoors may be all you need to boost creativity. Take time to notice what you see along the way in a whole new light.

YOU WILL NEED:

- paper and a writing utensil
- walking shoes
- your attention
- phone for taking photos, optional

1   Take a walk around the block, or to any 15-minute round-trip destination. While you are walking, take in your surroundings thoughtfully. Even if this is the same walk you've taken many times before, tune in. Notice the details, and really pay attention to all of the nuances happening around you.

2   As you walk, either scribble down a list or take pictures of twenty things you see. Do you think your list might change depending on your mood or your level of stress?

3   When you get home, scroll through your list or your photos and make little sketches. Fill up a page with walk details. Feel free to write and draw together to tell your story. Elaborate and embellish as much as you'd like.

Note: Try not to let documenting the walk take over the walk. Every time your mind wanders, or if you get overly hung up on taking a photo, just bring yourself back to your walk, and what is in front of you.

Collage Your Collection

Often, we collect things that have stories attached to them. With this exercise, honor your stories by organizing your items on a piece of mixed-media paper. You could paint the paper to give your collection a background that suits it. When choosing a collection, keep in mind that it can be a collection of any things that are tied together in some way. The connection between the items doesn't need to be apparent to anyone but you.

YOU WILL NEED:

- collection of things: some office supplies, a handful of rocks from your yard, stuff you find on a walk in the city, and so on

- piece of multimedia paper or board, any size

- camera of any kind

1   Decide on a collection of items to use for this exercise. Do you have a container of rocks you've collected at the beach? Or a collection of buttons in a jar? Maybe you have a bunch of matchbooks or rubber bands that you've been hanging onto.

2   The only rule is that there are no rules. Simply take your items (as many as will fit on a page) and arrange them until you find a composition that pleases you. Once you're satisfied, stand above your creation and take a photo. Then feel free to rearrange the collection and photograph it again. Play with it as much as you'd like.

Bring out other collections you might have and repeat this exercise. Does this activity breathe a little life into your treasures? Do they go back to their spots with a little more air around them? Sometimes organizing things has a very calming effect as you create unique compositions.

Catalog of Dots

Sometimes inspiration for your next project can be found in the seemingly mundane objects that are right before your eyes. That pile of junk mail or the stack of catalogs that came in yesterday's post provide most of what you'll need for this exercise.

YOU WILL NEED:

- catalogs or magazines—anything will work, even junk mail if it's colorful

- hole punches—a standard one is fine, but larger sizes are welcome

- glue stick or other craft glue

- heavy piece of paper to use as a base, any size

- matte gel medium

- paintbrush

1 Page through the catalogs and punch out some colorful dots. Be sure to include dots in neutral shades—whites and grays can offer a quiet space among colors.

2 When you have a good pile of dots, decide on an approach to your design. You might begin with, "I am going to make a multicolor cityscape out of dots," or you could begin more organically, by gluing down one dot at a time, making up the design as you go along.

3 Build up your image dot by dot. Punch out more dots in specific colors as you need them.

4 Once you have everything glued down, give your composition a fresh look. What do you like? What do you want to change? Add or remove dots to achieve the look you're after. When you're happy with it, gently brush gel matte medium over the entire design. Then punch out some more dots and start again!

Color Palette Explore

At its heart, color is personal. We all gravitate toward certain colors and even have favorites beginning when we are children. We know which ones appeal to us for an endless variety of reasons.

Imagine the way we respond to a beautiful expanse of very saturated green grass, contrasted with a bright blue sky. Can you recall a foggy day when everything was coated in a haze and you were in a sea of fuzzy neutral colors? We also respond to color palettes in works of art.

When it comes to making our own art, color can be simple or extremely complex. The way we play with color in this exercise—choosing colors that suggest a particular mood—is simple. There's no drawing involved, just thinking about color and choosing the ones we like. Play with the way colors work together and see if anything strikes you.

Because color is tied to mood and our moods can be somewhat fluid, you may find that what suits you one day may not feel right the next. Stay open and consider this exercise as a way to play and discover. You may learn a thing or two about context, including what one color does alongside another, as well as learning about your own preferences.

YOU WILL NEED:

- paint of your choice (acrylic, watercolor, gouache)

- markers of any kind

- mixed-media paper, watercolor paper, or a primed panel (any surface that will handle paint)

- paintbrushes, in a variety of sizes

1   Let's start with the word "calm." Do any colors come to mind? Try not to overthink it, just play. Paint or make swatches with colored pencils or markers. The goal is to add color to your page, see how you react, and notice how the colors react to one another.

2   Create a calm palette with three colors. Next, consider which neutrals to pair with them. Experiment with a few muted or neutral colors until you find two that fit well with your palette.

3   Continue this experiment, using any word or mood you can dream up. Just as you might imagine a soundtrack to a scene in a movie, you can create a feeling or mood in your artwork through color. Try the words "happy," "warm," and "winter." See which colors best represent these words. Create your own five-color palettes for each. (See A.)

If you wish, work up your palettes on smaller pieces of paper and keep them for reference. Did you come up with a palette that made you want to start a drawing? The palettes may be helpful references when you're starting a painting, prompting you to consider the mood or even season. Begin a catalog of color combinations that are personal to you. You might give each one a name and date, so you can compare your thoughts about color and mood on another day.

A

Circle Demonstrating Color Differences and Contrasts. From the book, *Expose d'un Moyen de definir et de nommer les couleurs,* by Eugene Chevreul. Published in Paris by Firmin Didot in 1861. Color lithograph. French school, nineteenth century. Private Collection/Archives Charmant/Bridgeman Images.

Lessons from the Color Wheel

Take a look at the color wheel. Colors that are next to one another are analogous, and tend to create a feeling of harmony or unity. Colors that are opposite one another on the wheel are complementary. Complementary colors feel vibrant and energetic when placed next to one another because of their contrast.

Use versions of complementary colors next to one another to create a palette that is a bit unexpected. Ultimately, color should convey your intent for whatever you might be making. Whether you're creating an autumn landscape; a calm, meditative drawing; or an energetic, upbeat piece that feels sunny and bright, you will have a sense of how the colors should feel. Once you become comfortable with the idea of using color to communicate, play with your options—they are endless!

ACKNOWLEDGMENTS

A heartfelt thanks to the stellar team at Quarry Books. Thank you to Mary Ann Hall, for giving me this lovely opportunity. Thank you to Judith Cressy, for your thoughtful editing, feedback, and support, which has been so helpful throughout this process. Thanks to Heather Godin, for your creative guidance and art direction, and to Mary Rockwood Lane, for adding your expertise to this project.

Thank you to Kelly, who always has brilliant ideas and when I am coming up a little short, and to Pat, for helping me find my way creatively for many moons.

To Linda, for drinking coffee with me, and for always understanding when I was trying to find my way. To Barb, who believed this was possible long before I ever believed it.

Thank you to my mom, Rosalie, for stepping in to help with the kids when I needed some focused work time, for your love and encouragement, and for keeping me caffeinated. Thank you to my Dad, Ray, and to Sandy, for your love and support. Thanks to my brother, Paul, for recommending Mindful Meditation a long time ago—I will have that tool forever. Thank you to my sister, Jill, for your constant encouragement and love. Thank you also to Ken and Pat, for your generosity—you have done so much to help us through the busiest times.

To Ryan, you are a wonderful husband and father, and this project would not have been possible without you. Thank you for your love, patience, and support. You are amazing, and I am grateful. Last, thank you to Tegan and Rocket, for your medicinal hugs. My hope is that you continue to find your calm through making art of all kinds.

ABOUT THE AUTHOR

Susan Evenson is a freelance artist and illustrator, photo art director, wife, mom, daughter, sister, and friend. She has been exploring meditation and yoga for several years and is always looking for ways to weave these practices together with her art making. She enjoys painting, drawing in sketchbooks, making dream maps, and making collaborative paintings with her daughter. This is her very first book.

INDEX